Colonel Marshall Lefferts

The Regiment That Saved the Capital

By
William J. Roehrenbeck,

Introduction by **Allan Nevins**

New York·Thomas Yoseloff·London

Thomas Yoseloff, Publisher
11 East 36th Street
New York 16, New York

Thomas Yoseloff Ltd.
123 New Bond Street
London W. 1, England

The jacket illustration is a reproduction of Thomas Nast's painting, "The March Down Broadway," depicting the departure from New York of the Seventh Regiment. Nast's painting is on permanent exhibit in the Seventh Regiment Armory, Sixty-sixth Street and Park Avenue, New York City.

Preface

MILITARY GLORY ordinarily accrues to a regiment as a result
of battlefield honors. The tattered battle flags, the trophies,
the old weapons, and the mementoes are cherished where-
ever the "old boys" of the regiment gather to relive the
days of their youth. In the Civil War, the Seventh Regiment New York State Militia (now the 107th Infantry
New York National Guard) was not destined to fight under
its own colors in any major engagement. Yet, in a manner
more subtle but none the less substantial, it made a notable
contribution to the Union cause and won for itself lasting
glory. At a moment of national peril, the Seventh, almost to
a man and with only a handful of new recruits, packed up
within a few hours and marched off to relieve the National
Capital. As the model militia regiment of the nation it
helped to provide the spark that lit the fires of patriotism
in those early days. As a natural training school for officers
it was to see over six hundred of its members achieve distinction in other units.

This is the story of its forty-five days of active service:
from April 19 to June 3, 1861. It is the story of a thousand
young men, most of them socially prominent, wealthy, and
highly placed in New York businesses and professions, who
dropped everything at the President's call and hustled off to

save Washington. They had no way of knowing what they faced, but they had no doubts that they were marching with the best regiment in the Union and were going to prove it in the days ahead.

Fortunately, the sources of information about the Regiment are plentiful. By 1860 the Seventh had come into national prominence and the newspapers of various cities were giving full coverage to their activities. In fact, it is difficult to escape the impression that, from the point of view of public-relations, the early federalization of the Seventh was a key move in the mobilization plans of the North. Most of the present account is based on two regimental histories, one by Emmons B. Clark and one by William Swinton, supplemented by the delightful reports of Theodore Winthrop and Fitz-James O'Brien. The *Official Records of the Rebellion* and various documents of the State of New York have been used extensively. A complete list of sources is available in the bibliography.

The author has received considerable help in the preparation of this volume, and he acknowledges it gratefully. Lt. Col. John F. Carroll, who is a former company commander of B Company, generously placed his collection of manuscripts and illustrations at the author's disposal and gave much-needed advice at every stage. Mr. Charles Gosnell, the state librarian of New York, was most helpful in providing manuscript materials. Thanks are also due to the staff of the New-York Historical Society for their courtesy in allowing the use of the extensive military library of the Seventh Regiment on deposit there; to Capt. Victor Gondos of the National Archives; to Mr. O. C. Dornbusch of the New York Public Library; and to Col. James M. Stewart, present commander of the Regiment.

W.J.R.

Introduction

ANY REGIMENT in the world might envy the Seventh of New York some pages of its history. In its long record from 1806, when it was formed as a unit of the Volunteer Militia, to the present day, when it is part of the National Guard to which it gave the official name, it has no page which requires excuse. Through three great wars and in minor conflicts it has done memorable service. The spirit and tradition of the Seventh, meanwhile, have been of constant importance. In a country which has always distrusted standing armies, it has demonstrated the possibility of uniting strict discipline and professional expertness with the volunteer impulse and amateur background. This thorough and objective volume does justice to one chapter in its record.

The most celebrated day in the annals of the Seventh, April 25, 1861, is mentioned in every detailed account of the Civil War, and finds at least a note in every full history of our literature. It is remembered by war historians because it marked the sudden emergence of the National Capital from a period of peril and dread into the light of security and hopefulness; and it is interesting to literary students because one of the regiment's young officers, Major Theodore Winthrop, penned a narrative of its southward journey that maintains a place in anthologies of American prose. While other forces were still preparing, the Seventh was ready to press to the relief of Washington—and none too soon. A secessionist mob dominated Baltimore; the direct rail line had been cut; Maryland still hesitated between treason and loyalty. Heavy Virginia forces were reported at hand to swoop down upon President and Cabinet, half protected, as this volume shows, by a flimsy military screen, which had been thinly reinforced by the Sixth Massachusetts.

Seldom has so much suspense hung upon the progress of one regiment. The Seventh set forth from a city seething with excitement. The diarist George Templeton Strong has stirringly described its departure; a bluish steel-gray rivulet moving from far up Broadway down to the Battery, between dense banks of spectators whose roar drowned out the band, their flags thrashing, their handkerchiefs waving. Everywhere, men were drilling; the Eighth, the Thirteenth, and the Sixty-ninth Regiments were also about to leave for the front; the city council was voting a million for initial war expenses; the mayor and council were tendering a reception to the defender of Fort Sumter, Major Robert Anderson; a huge flag had been flung from Trinity steeple; a future President, Chester A. Arthur, as assistant state quartermaster, was erecting a building in City Hall Park to feed fifteen hundred soldiers at a time; mass meetings, including one of mammoth size in Union Square, were being held. Tumultuous days! But would the Seventh, moving roundabout by Annapolis, reach Washington in time? On the morning of the twenty-fifth General Winfield Scott was writing orders to warn the city of an attack next day:

Then, at noon, a mighty shout came from the Sixth Massachusetts encamped on Capitol Hill. They had seen a troop train drawing into the station. Citizens began running pell-mell to the scene. As the train stopped a wild burst of cheering was heard even at the Treasury. Under a bright sun, the trim ranks of the Seventh were soon marching up Pennsylvania Avenue, whose sidewalks filled magically. The men kept soldierly step under their unstained banners, and when their band struck up onlookers danced with delight. On they came, past Willard's, past the Treasury, through the White House grounds, and under the very eaves of the mansion. Lincoln emerged to wave them a greeting, the happiest-looking man in town. As an Illinois man remarked, "He smiled all over."

The Regiment's feat was the more remarkable because in getting to Washington its members had to turn their hands to unwonted work. "Men used to Wall Street, Park Place, the Fifth Avenue, and Bloomingdale Road," as Greeley's *Tribune* said, converted themselves into navvies to rebuild the Annapolis-Washington railroad. This silk-stocking unit had been the object of no little derision as being more interested in fashion than fighting. "Why is the Seventh Regiment like Lord Nelson?" George Templeton Strong had asked in 1860. "Because its last act would be to die for its country." But now men jested at it no more.

Ahead lay four grim years, in which men of the Seventh played a gallant and varied part. The Regiment helped guard Washington for three months, setting an example to raw outfits—as it had given Ellsworth an example in forming his own crack company—by its decorum, neatness, and proficiency in drill and tactics. It was called into service again when Stonewall Jackson swept up the Shenandoah in 1862, and when Lee marched to Gettysburg, this latter tour of duty being shortened when the Regiment was called back to help quell the Draft Riots. Hundreds of the men, however, scattered as officers into other units, did sterling work on grim fields. Three of them won Congressional Medals. One, Egbert L. Viele, was with Lincoln on the only occasion a President of the United States commanded troops in the field. Another, Fitz-James O'Brien, had his promising career as officer and author cut short by a bullet in a West Virginia skirmish. Still another, Robert Gould Shaw of Staten Island, immortalized himself by his leadership of the famous Negro regiment, the Fifty-fourth Massachusetts, meeting his death at Fort Wagner near Charleston. Had New York possessed a John A. Andrew instead of a Horatio Seymour as Governor, that regiment, recruited all over the East, might have fought under an Empire State designation.

"The most thorough militia regiment in existence," Theodore Winthrop termed the Seventh; its mere name carried weight. This volume, as restrained as the Regiment is disciplined, as careful in fact and interpretation as the Regiment is in *tenue* and deportment, and as filled with a spirit of true patriotism as the men led by Marshall Lefferts and Emmons Clark, is a valuable contribution to the commemoration of the Civil War.

ALLAN NEVINS

CONTENTS

ILLUSTRATIONS

To Jean

I Washington and New York on the Verge of War

ON THAT SUNDAY MORNING the President of the United States met in the White House with a grim-faced cabinet and a flustered array of the top-level military. It was April 14, 1861, and the moment had now come when Mr. Lincoln had to preside at the climax of the dramatic sequence which he had set in motion two weeks ago. Down in Charleston the bishop of the Episcopal diocese declared that "the movement in which the people were engaged was begun by them in the deepest conviction of duty to God," and at the same time the Roman Catholic bishop celebrated a *Te Deum* in his cathedral.[1] Sumter had fallen and the President now had to step firmly into his role as "Commander-in-chief of the Army and Navy of the United States, and of the militia of the several States." Looking backward, the inevitability of this moment is crystal clear. A point of no return had been reached, perhaps as early as the election in November 1860; or on December 20 when South Carolina adopted its ordinance of secession; perhaps, on March 4 when Lincoln was inaugurated amid martial trappings. At some point the Nation had veered off the road

to peaceful settlement and now could not turn back. Ten
days ago, on April 4, when the President made the decision
to reinforce Fort Sumter, he set off a chain reaction which
would bring him inexorably to the time when he would
have to issue a presidential call to arms. The intervening
events had been logical and inevitable: Beauregard's order
to open fire on the twelfth, the thirty-four-hour bombardment, and Anderson's surrender at seven P.M. on April 13.
Civil war had begun and with it the task of arming the
Nation.

The city itself was in a turmoil of bewilderment and
apprehension. Ever since Inauguration Day, when, for the
first time in history, troops had lined Pennsylvania Avenue,
Washington had been tense with expectancy. Uneasiness
alternated with moments of calm, as each day brought new
reports and rumors. News had been trickling into the city
about the bombardment late Friday and all day Saturday.
Now, early Sunday morning, the whole town was aware
that Major Anderson had surrendered his garrison. All at
once the heights of Arlington across the river looked
ominous and forbidding. It was not difficult to imagine rebel
columns tramping across Long Bridge and the Georgetown
aqueduct. Not even the Seventh Street road and Bladensburg Turnpike, leading through doubtful Maryland to the
North, could be trusted. A sizable exodus had begun. De-
parting trains were filled with those anxious to get out before the rebels made an attack, most of them office-seekers
who had been bedevilling Lincoln since his inauguration.
In Willard's Hotel at Fourteenth Street and throughout
Georgetown, a stronghold of disunion, secession sympathizers were delighting in the boasts of Southern jour-
nalists and rumors of rapid Confederate arming. The
District militia had been called out and were placed on

guard duty at the public buildings. At all the approaches to Washington, pickets of United States Cavalry were posted. It was an atmosphere of siege, the first of the war, and it was to last until April 25 when Northern troops came marching in.

The difficulties facing the administration in organizing for war were little short of breathtaking. To begin with, the Government was less than two months old. At this point they were still at the stage of handing out jobs and assigning office space. To mount a major war effort, they would need to work as a team and they were far from this achievement. Their difficulties were most noticeable in two particular areas. The Treasury had been hard hit by the withdrawal of seven states from the Union, and there was going to be a need for heavy borrowing and taxation in order to sustain the necessary land and naval forces. Later in the year, Salmon P. Chase, secretary of the Treasury, had to ask for $320,000,000, of which $80,000,000 was to be raised by taxation and the remainder by borrowing. For these bonds the government would have to pay 7 per cent interest. Thus, any decision about raising an army would have to be scrutinized very carefully in the light of financial capability.

More important was the condition of the Nation's defenses. The people of the United States were, quite simply, unwarlike. At the close of the War of the Revolution they had flung aside Washington's army and allowed the Nation's military strength to dwindle to one regiment and a battalion of artillery. As the country expanded, the Regular Army was increased in size to meet different crises, but always there was the basic opposition to a large standing army. Wars, if they had to be fought, should be fought by the citizenry, called to serve their country in moments of crisis. Thus, Congress had early recognized the principle that every able-bodied citizen should be an active defender of his country. The universal militia law of 1792 made every male citizen between the ages of eighteen and forty-five a potential soldier. The law, however, was mostly ignored from the moment of its passage. There was no penalty for the failure of a state to raise troops, nor on an individual citizen for neglecting to provide himself with the weapons specified in the law. Thus, the state militias in 1860 were made up of volunteer military organizations of varying merit and independence, most of them barely able to shoulder arms, much less go out on field service. Stories were spread gleefully about the blunders of officers who marched their regiments up to a high wall before they could remember how to stop them. In the eastern cities most people had never even seen a company of the Regular Army. Furthermore, although the South had already started active preparations for war and its men were drilling, the Northern mind could not quite comprehend the onrushing crisis and definitely shrank from the belief that war was possible.

On April 5 the Adjutant-General of the United States Army had reported to the President that the entire Regular Army consisted of 17,113 officers and men, of whom only 3,894 were in the Department of the East and the remainder scattered throughout the various western Departments.[2] Within a few days 313 of the officers would resign their commissions and depart for the South. The Navy was in an equally weakened condition. Its total force was 1,457 officers and 7,600 men scattered all over the world, with less than half of its ninety ships ready for active service. Defections to the South were to be disastrous also in this branch of the service. In all, the Navy lost 16 captains, 34 commanders, 76 lieutenants, and 111 regular and acting midshipmen.

Along with these two basic difficulties, financial and military, there was uncertainty as to the duration of the war. At this point no one could safely predict whether it was necessary to arm for a long struggle, or whether the rebellion would crumble at the first show of Northern force. The prevailing opinion until after the debacle at Bull Run in July was that it would be a short war. In fact, Chase's whole plan for financing the war was based on this assumption, and Congress accepted his estimate by enacting his proposals on July 17. If anyone had a clear concept of the difficulties ahead, it was probably old Winfield Scott, General-in-chief of the Army. A hero of the War of 1812 and the Mexican War, he knew how long it took to recruit and train a volunteer army. He also had learned his lessons in strategy and within a month was able to produce his Anaconda plan, which proposed strangling the Confederacy by seizure of the Mississippi from Cairo to the Gulf, along with a blockade of all Southern ports. Despite the ridicule heaped on this plan because it presumed a long major war effort, it became the basic strategy of the Federal Government.

The spectre of losing the border states to the South was, of course, always present in every discussion at this stage and had a profound influence on all policy decisions. Would Delaware, Maryland, Virginia, Missouri, Kentucky, and Tennessee remain loyal to the Union or join the other slave states? If all of them seceded, the position was hopeless. It was probable, however, that Missouri, Kentucky, and Tennessee could be held if Federal troops were sent there promptly. Virginia and Maryland presented the most immediate problems. Virginia was, after all, only a few thousand feet away across the Potomac. The situation in this state had in fact been the key to the timetable of events during the last month. Lincoln's delay in sending reinforcements to Sumter was based primarily on his fear that he might drive Virginia out of the Union by doing so. On the Confederate side also, one of the major factors influencing the decision to open hostilities was the conviction that secessionist feeling would harden if a blow were struck by her sister-states of the South. By April 12 it was safe to predict secession within a few days, despite strong support for the Federal Government in the western part of the state and the previous reluctance of Governor Letcher to leave the Union. While it was possible to write off Virginia as a loss, the same was not true of Maryland. The state surrounded the District of Columbia on three sides. Baltimore was the junction of three railroads and held the key to communication with the North. The state was probably safe with Governor Hicks pro-Union. It would have to be watched carefully, however, because secessionist sentiment ran high, particularly in Baltimore, and there was always the possibility that the state government would be swept before it. Thus Lincoln and his advisers had been walking very gingerly in all their pre-Sumter movements, lest they alienate these critical areas.

As Lincoln expressed it several weeks later in an interview with members of New York's Seventh Regiment, three things had to be done quickly: "defend Washington, blockade the ports, and retake government property." [3] Of these, the defense of the city was of immediate concern on April 14, for there were definite signs that Washington was in a decidedly precarious position and would be until more troops were brought in. The eyes of the South naturally turned to the capital on the Potomac as the main prize to be won. Southern newspapers were filled with confident predictions of the capture of the District. In Montgomery,

Leroy P. Walker, Confederate Secretary of War, envisioned the rebel flag flying over Washington before the first of May. William H. Russell, correspondent of the London *Times*, cabled his newspaper that an attack was expected. As early as January 2, *The New York Times* had reported the existence in Maryland and Virginia of military companies formed for the express purpose of aiding in the seizure of Washington. Ben McCulloch, the famous Texas Ranger, was reported to be in Richmond ready to lead an attack. In the light of this particular threat, the District of Columbia militia had been ordered to assemble at their armories on April 11. Lincoln himself had been receiving warnings. On April 13, James Henderson wrote him from New York:

> I am in receipt of information, the authenticity of which I cannot doubt, that the secession leaders intend to make a sudden and desperate attempt to seize Washington City. When and how the attempt will be made is not known positively outside the city of Montgomery, but as I communicated to Gen. Scott yesterday, the intention to make such attempt exists, and practical means for that purpose are being consumated [sic] by paid Agents at Washington city, and the cities of Virginia and Maryland, and here at New York.[4]

While many of these threats, at a later date, were found to be rumors, the potential of a Confederate attack in the weeks following the fall of Sumter was most real and alarming. The impending secession of Virginia placed the enemy only a few feet across the Potomac. The hostility of Maryland and its ardent secessionist element meant that Baltimore might be seized and communication thus cut off with the North.

Scott, meanwhile, had been moving as many regular

troops into the city as possible. In his daily reports to the President he did not appear too alarmed about the weakness of his defenses. As late as April 5 he saw no need for Lincoln to call out the militia but changed abruptly on April 9 and asked that ten companies of the District of Columbia militia, or volunteers, be supplied to guard government buildings. At Fort Washington, a broken-down installation ten miles below the city on the banks of the Potomac opposite Mount Vernon, he had a garrison of fifty recruits. At the Navy Yard some two hundred Marines were stationed who could be counted on for service. Despite all his efforts and his implied optimism he had a mere handful of men on hand at the outbreak of war. On the thirteenth he reported:

> . . . At my instance the Secretary of War has called for four other companies of District volunteers, which will make in all fifteen companies of this description for the defense of the Capital, besides six companies of regulars, the marines at the navy yard, and (I hope very soon) the war steamer to cruise on the Potomac between the long bridge and a point a little below Alexandria. The next regular reënforcements to be expected here are: Sherman's battery of flying artillery from Minnesota, and the companies of foot artillery from the same quarter, in five and seven days; and a portion of the troops expected in the next steamer from Texas. . . .[5]

Against this background the conferees met at the White House to work out the details of action. In such an emergency the President's course of action was clearly indicated. An insurrection was in existence; government property had been seized illegally; the National Capital was in danger. The militia of the various states must therefore be called out and troops brought to Washington as quickly as pos-

sible. Congress, however, was not in session, and, under
the Constitution, the power to call forth the militia and
provide for its organization, arming, and discipline rested
in that body. Thus, if the rebellion could not be crushed
quickly, the major call for volunteers would have to wait
until Congress could be called into session. The President,
however, did have power under the militia act of February
28, 1795, to call out the militias of the states in an emergency. Accordingly, Lincoln had a proclamation already
prepared for discussion on the fourteenth.

The major restriction in the 1795 legislation concerned
the term of service of militia so summoned by the President. Congress had to be convened directly and the use of
militia was authorized only "until the expiration of thirty
days after the commencement of the then next session of
Congress." For many reasons it seemed wise to the Administration to defer an extra session of Congress until July 4.
As a result the term of service for troops called up under the
proclamation was fixed at three months. As to the number
of troops needed, Lincoln proposed 75,000. Apparently he
had some difficulty in arriving at the proper figure and
later ran into some heavy criticism as to the adequacy of
the call. Actually, on May 3 he had to issue a supplementary
call for 42,000 three-year volunteers and a sizable increase
in the Regular Army and Navy. At the time, however, on
April 14 he had to take into consideration the shortage of
funds, the state of public opinion, which had been far from
enthusiastic during the past few weeks, and the ever-
present problem of alienating the border states. According
to his secretaries,

> . . . eleventh hour critics continue to insist that a larger
> force should have been called at once. They forget that this
> was nearly five times the then existing regular army; that

only very limited quantities of arms, equipments, and supplies were in the Northern arsenals; that the treasury was bankrupt. . . . They forget that the shameful events of the past four months had elicited scarcely a spark of war feeling. . . . Even that number appeared a hazardous experiment—an immense army, a startling expenditure. As matters stood it seemed enough to cope with the then visible forces of the rebellion. . . .[6]

Whatever doubts he may have had, Lincoln, nevertheless, with the concurrence of his cabinet, had the following proclamation copied immediately and sent to the State Department for publication on the following day, April 15, 1861:

BY THE PRESIDENT OF THE UNITED STATES: A PROCLAMATION

Whereas the laws of the United States have been for some time past and now are opposed and the execution thereof obstructed in the States of South Carolina, Georgia, Alabama, Florida, Mississippi, Louisiana, and Texas by combinations too powerful to be suppressed by the ordinary course of judicial proceedings or by the powers vested in the marshals by law:

Now, therefore, I, Abraham Lincoln, President of the United States, in virtue of the power in me vested by the Constitution and the laws, have thought fit to call forth, and hereby do call forth, the militia of the several States of the Union, to the aggregate number of 75,000, in order to suppress said combinations and to cause the laws to be duly executed.

The details of this object will be immediately communicated to the State authorities through the War Department.

I appeal to all loyal citizens to favor, facilitate, and aid this effort to maintain the honor, the integrity, and the existence of our National Union, and the perpetuity of popular government, and to redress wrongs already long enough endured.

I deem it proper to say that the first service assigned to the forces hereby called forth will probably be to repossess the forts, places, and property which have been seized from the Union, and in every event the utmost care will be observed, consistently with objects aforesaid, to avoid any devastation, any destruction of, or interference with property, or any disturbance of peaceful citizens in any part of the country.

And I hereby command the persons composing the combinations aforesaid to disperse and retire peaceably to their respective abodes within twenty days from date.

Deeming that the present condition of public affairs presents an extraordinary occasion, I do hereby in virtue of the power vested in me by the Constitution, convene both houses of Congress.

Senators and Representatives are therefore summoned to assemble at their respective chambers at twelve o'clock noon on Thursday, the fourth of July next, then and there to consider and determine such measures as in their wisdom the public safety and interest may seem to demand.

In witness thereof I have hereunto set my hand and caused the seal of the United States to be affixed.

Done at the city of Washington this fifteenth day of April, in the year of our Lord one thousand eight hundred and sixty-one, and of the Independence of the United States the eighty-fifth.

                          ABRAHAM LINCOLN
By the President

                          WILLIAM H. SEWARD
                            Secretary of State[7]

In order to implement this proclamation, Secretary Cameron immediately notified the governors of the various states by telegraph that a requisition was being made and sent to each of them the following letter:

WAR DEPARTMENT
Washington, April 15, 1861.

SIR: Under the act of Congress "for calling forth the militia to execute the laws of the Union, suppress insurrections, repel invasions," &c., approved February 28, 1795, I have the honor to request Your Excellency to cause to be immediately detached from the militia of your State the quota designated in the table below, to serve as infantry or riflemen, for the period of three months, unless sooner discharged.

Your Excellency will please communicate to me the time at or about which your quota will be expected at its rendezvous, as it will be met as soon as practicable by an officer or officers to muster it into the service and pay of the United States. At the same time the oath of fidelity to the United States will be administered to every officer and man. The mustering officer will be instructed to receive no man under the rank of commissioned officer who is in years apparently over forty-five or under eighteen, or who is not in physical strength and vigor. . . .

I have the honor to be, very respectfully, your obedient servant,

SIMON CAMERON
Secretary of War.[8]

Included in the communication was a table of quotas and a list of the rendezvous points. According to this table New York was called upon for seventeen regiments of 649 officers and 12,631 men, a total force of 13,280. In addition, two major-generals and four brigadier-generals were specified.

The response was immediate and most of the Northern governors rushed to be the first with troops. Andrew, of

Massachusetts, who had been preparing for this moment for some time replied, "Dispatch received. By what route shall we send?" Curtin, of Pennsylvania, wanted to know if Cameron would accept the Ringgold Artillerists of Reading who had already started "and were very superior in men and drill." Morgan, of New York, whose Legislature was ready to adjourn on the sixteenth, did not wait for the Secretary of War's official notice listing the quotas but immediately pushed through legislation providing for men and money for public defense. The border states, however, reacted with varying degrees of dudgeon. Ellis, of North Carolina, which had not yet left the Union, said, "I can be no party to this wicked violation of the laws of the country and to this war upon the liberties of a free people. You can get no troops from North Carolina." Magoffin, of Kentucky, stated emphatically, "Kentucky will furnish no troops for the wicked purpose of subduing her sister Southern States." Letcher, of Virginia, doubted the "genuineness of the telegram" and insisted that "your object is to subjugate the Southern States, and a requisition made upon me for such an object—an object, in my judgment, not within the purview of the Constitution or the act of 1795—will not be complied with." In Tennessee, Harris replied that he "will not furnish a single man for purposes of coercion, but 50,000, if necessary, for the defense of our rights and those of our Southern brethren," and in Missouri, Jackson vowed that "not one man will the State of Missouri furnish to carry on such an unholy crusade." Maryland wanted to be certain that its troops would be used only for the defense of the Capital. Delaware waited ten days and then announced that it had no organized militia, but that volunteer troops were being raised within the state.[9]

The alacrity of this response was a reflection of the phenomenal outburst of emotion that had been sweeping through the North since April 12, when the first news of the showdown at Sumter began to come over the telegraph wires. The declining months of Buchanan's administration and the uncertainty of governmental policy since Lincoln's inauguration produced nothing but apathy and gloom. George Templeton Strong, the noted lawyer and diarist, sums it up forcefully in his entry for March 12:

> But, whoever may be responsible for the calamity, this is a time of sad humiliation for the country. Every citizen of what has heretofore been called the Great Republic of America, every man, woman, and child, from Maine to Texas, from Massachusetts to California, stands lower among the inhabitants of this earth tonight than in March, 1860. We are a weak, divided, disgraced people, unable to maintain our national existence. We are impotent even to assert our national life. The country of George Washington and Andrew Jackson (!!!) is decomposing, and its elements reforming into new and strange combinations.[10]

Overnight the picture changed. The blow at Sumter showed inescapably the determination of Southern leaders to resist any move toward reunion, and a tidal wave of anger and patriotism rolled over every city and village of the Union. Within hours the Nation was a beehive of bustling activity. Volunteer companies were being recruited and started drilling; special services were held in the churches; union meetings were scheduled; the resolutions started pouring out from every organization; business firms subscribed to funds, while legislatures raced to put through war appropriations. And nowhere was there more bustle than in New York City.

The changing picture of New York during April 1861

is apparent in every newspaper account of the period. However, under the shrewd, perceptive pen of G. T. Strong, who knew and loved his city thoroughly, the story comes to life vividly. He had voted for Lincoln and expected great things from him. During the early months of 1861 he was much concerned and pessimistic over the inaction and uncertainty. His depression began to lift, however, on Monday, April 8, when he visited the Brooklyn Navy Yard and found that "a large force sailed on Saturday for parts unknown, but there is still great bustle and activity there, getting the *Wabash* and other ships ready for sea. Went on board the old *North Carolina* and came off after an interesting two hours, convinced that something is about to be done." Lincoln had ordered the reinforcement of Sumter on the fourth and the Navy was beginning to move.

On the ninth he reveals that many in the city were convinced that the fleet was "destined for Charleston harbor, and that Fort Sumter is not to be given up after all." On the following day the *Tribune* and the *Times* confirmed the news, and New York, with the rest of the Nation, began its vigil.

Strong got the news of the bombardment of Sumter from the extra edition of the *Herald* on Friday, the twelfth, and "doubts its genuineness vehemently. I can hardly hope that the rebels have been so foolish and thoughtless as to take the initiative in civil war and bring matters to a crisis." The next day, New York had a confirmation of the news, and Strong comments on the changed attitude.

The Northern backbone is much stiffened already. Many who stood up for "Southern rights" and complained of wrongs done the South now say that, since the South has fired the first gun, they are ready to go all lengths in supporting the government. The New York *Herald* is non-

committal this morning. It may well be upholding the
Administration and denouncing the Democratic party
within a week.

Sunday morning's papers announced the surrender of
Sumter and the alarm was reflected in church services
throughout the city. Strong comments on the number of
prominent Democrats who are now supporting the Government and states that "If this class of men has been secured
and converted to loyalty, the gain to the country is worth
ten Sumters." On the fifteenth came the news of Lincoln's
proclamation and the call for 75,000 volunteers.

The New York *Herald* on Monday, April 15, was "just at
the turning point" and with it the *Express*. The *Journal of
Commerce*, however, "shows no signs of reformation yet."
Evidently the war fever in New York was beginning to
shoot upward sharply at this point, because the *Herald* was
already being threatened with attack. James Gordon Ben-
nett, its publisher, suddenly found himself most unpopular
with New Yorkers who would not tolerate even slight traces
of non-conformism. "This brazen old scoundrel was hooted
up Fulton Street yesterday afternoon [Monday] by a mob,
and the police interfered to prevent it from sacking his
printing office."

On the seventeenth there was more violence. As Strong
recalls:

> I was sitting in my office at three o'clock when I heard
> unwonted sounds in Wall Street, and looking out, saw a
> straggling column of men running toward the East River.
> My first notion was that they were chasing a runaway horse,
> but they soon became too numerous to be engaged in that.
> They halted in front of the *Journal of Commerce* office and
> filled the street densely for about a block. There were out-
> cries, which I could not distinctly hear for a minute, and

then the American flag was hung out from a window, and the crowd sent up a cheer that stirred one's blood a little, and the surface of the black mass was suddenly all in motion with waving hats. Then a line of policemen came down the street on a dogtrot, and the crowd thereupon moved promptly up Wall Street again, cheering lustily.

They were mostly decently-dressed people, but with a sprinkling of laboring men. I understand they paid a like domiciliary visit to the *Express*, the *Day-Book* and the *Daily News*, requiring each to put up the flag. They intended to call on the New York Hotel, it is said, but Cranston was forewarned and the American flag was flying from its roof as I came uptown.

On the eighteenth Strong watched the Sixth Massachusetts Regiment march down Broadway, his eyes "filled with tears" and "half choked in sympathy with the contagious excitement." It then occurred to him that the flag should be flying from the tower of Trinity Church—"an unprecedented demonstration, but these are unprecedented times." He had some misgivings, but to his surprise General Dix, Cisco Skidmore, Swift, and Gouverneur Ogden, agreed with him and joined in signing a note asking Dr. Berrian, the rector, for permission. Strong expected a refusal from the rector, "supported by platitudes of fogyism, easily to be imagined." At dinner a note came from the rector who "very cheerfully complies with our request. Hurrah for Dr. Berrian! His consent to this is the strongest indication yet of the intensity of our national feeling just now. May we dare to hope it will last?" That night, Strong went to the Brevoort House where Major Anderson was staying. He had arrived in New York in the afternoon with his command. A large crowd was there, cheering for Anderson and groaning for James Watson Webb, who had attacked Anderson for his conduct, in the *Courier and Enquirer*.

On the following morning he continued his flag-raising project.

> Busy this morning in pursuit of a flag for Trinity Church steeple. Hunted through the city with Vinton in vain; went off on my own account and secured one at last (20 by 40) from Robert B. Minturn, who was most kind and obliging. He went to one of his ships with me and insisted on sending up riggers to help Secor's people hoist it. At half-past two, it went up; the chimes saluting it with "Hail Columbia," "Yankee Doodle," and "Old Hundred," and a crowd in Wall Street and Broadway cheering. Higby, Vinton and Ogilby led the cheers. The flinging out of the flag, the clang of the Bells, and the enthusiastic cheering, gave me a new sensation. I am amazed by the strong feeling of gratification strengthened by surprise that this little flourish called out.

In the afternoon he watched the parade of the Seventh Regiment, which sent New York into its greatest frenzy of the week and on Saturday, the twentieth, attended the Union mass-meeting in Union Square. The newspapers claimed an attendance of 250,000, which Strong thought was probably an exaggeration. As he describes the approach to Union Square and the meeting itself:

> Walked uptown at two. Broadway crowded and more crowded as one approached Union Square. Large companies of recruits in citizen's dress parading up and down cheered and cheering. Small mobs around the headquarters of the regiments that are going to Washington, staring at the sentinel on duty. Every other man, woman, and child bearing a flag or decorated with a cockade. Flags from almost every building. The city seems to have gone suddenly wild and crazy.
>
> The Union mass-meeting was an event. Few assemblages have equalled it in numbers and unanimity. Tonight's extra

says there were 250,000 present. That must be an exaggeration. But the multitude was enormous. All the area bounded by Fourteenth and Seventeenth Streets, Broadway and Fourth Avenue, was filled. In many places it was densely packed, and nowhere could one push his way without difficulty.[11]

Thus, New York, the "big town," with all the exuberance of a pack of cowhands riding into Abilene after a month on the range, put aside its gloom and plunged into war. Overnight the city had turned itself into a vast recruiting station. With a minimum of planning and complete lack of coordination, prominent citizens announced proposals to form regiments or companies, a recruiting station would be opened, and within a few days the quota would be raised. Dan Sickles formed the Excelsior Brigade; Abraham Duryea, the Advance Guard Zouaves; Elmer E. Ellsworth, the New York Fire Zouaves, made up entirely of city firemen. The Irish, the Germans, the Poles, and the Italians soon had their own regiments. The College of the City of New York, then the Free Academy, formed a company of Zouaves.

And, over in Tompkins Square, there was even greater scurrying, but more orderly and efficient. All New York was on the alert. The Seventh Regiment, the "darling" of the city and the Nation, had been ordered to Washington and was preparing to move out.

II The Seventh Regiment: Its Background and Organization

In the vast conglomerate of military organizations known as the organized militia of the several states of the Union, the Seventh Regiment New York State Militia stood out as the model for all others to imitate. Their discipline was rigid; their drill had a snap to it that few other units could achieve; their gray uniforms, with the immaculate white cross-belts, sparkled as they paraded down Broadway; their band was superb and in constant demand; the men themselves came from the "best" families in New York and thus created an aura of great wealth about the whole organization. The New York newspapers worshiped them and faithfully recounted the details of their parades, excursions, and summer encampments. Lately their reputation had become national. Almost every year since 1843 they had been visiting various cities of the East, and each trip, with all the attendant ceremonies and good-will, added to this reputation. The climax came in 1858 when they were chosen by the Common Council, "provided they bear their own expenses," to escort the remains of President Monroe from New York to Richmond, Virginia. There they were feted by the city government and entertained royally by the Richmond Grays among mutual pledges of undying friendship. Assignments such as this, and many others, only enhanced their prestige still more, and it became obvious that, in the coming days of crisis, their movements would be watched carefully.

The Seventh belonged to that long chain of volunteer corps that stretched back to the early days of Massachusetts Bay Colony: the Burgher Corps of New Amsterdam, and the Minutemen of pre-Revolutionary times. The colonial towns had discovered that they needed protection from raiding Indians, and each town formed its independent military corps for this purpose. The danger of Indian raids was long since past, but internal disorders continued and the local police forces often needed help in putting down riots. Besides, these volunteer groups were invaluable as a source of officers in times of national crisis.

The Volunteer Militia, the forerunner of the National Guard, must not be confused with the ordinary militia that operated in the early days of the Republic under the laws that required every able-bodied citizen to render military service. They were not professional soldiers; they were not draftees; they were not citizen wartime volunteers. The man who joined a volunteer company did so because he was interested in military affairs and was seeking the society of others with similar interests. The companies, or battalions, or regiments were independent military societies who were available to the State in times of emergency. They elected their own officers, designed and purchased their own uniforms, set up their own schedule of drills. Operating under a state military code, they were usually incorporated into brigades and together formed the military forces of the state government.

The members of the Seventh Regiment joined for a seven year period. They were accepted, not into the Regiment as a whole, but into a particular company of the Regiment. Dues were paid to the company, which shared with the other companies the cost of operating the Regiment. Fines were levied for non-attendance at drill, and special assessments were made for excursions and encampment. The member paid for his own uniforms. Company drills were held once a week, and, in addition, attendance at business meetings was required. The member did receive some benefits from the state. He was exempt from jury and military duty for life, once he had served seven years, and he received a five hundred dollar deduction from any city assessment for taxes on real or personal property.

The Seventh was a highly successful regiment, and a good part of this success was due to its standards of selection. The companies would accept only the best of the many applicants for admission. This meant that the ranks were filled with successful business and professional men who took pride in sustaining the traditions of excellence. It also ensured the election of sound officers who could provide top-level leadership. To become a member of the Seventh was almost the same as being admitted to an exclusive club. Thus it was not at all unusual to find ex-Regular Army officers, many of them West Point graduates, marching in the ranks as privates.

The story of the Regiment begins back in April 1806, when three British warships appeared off Sandy Hook and started to board and search all vessels entering New York Harbor. Unfortunately, they fired on the sloop *Richard* and killed the helmsman, John Pierce, a well-known and respected citizen of New York, whose death led to a series of indignation meetings. It also brought on the formation of a number of military organizations, to which the young men of the city clamored for admission. Among these new volunteer groups were four artillery companies which later became the first four companies of the Seventh Regiment. They were organized during May and June 1806 and, on July 25, were assigned to Sitcher's Battalion of Artillery, with the understanding that the battalion would be raised to a regiment as soon as the Legislature approved. The following year the four companies became the Second Battalion of the Third New York Artillery Regiment. In 1812 this was redesignated as the Eleventh Regiment of Artillery and the four companies became the Second Infantry Battalion.

For some time prior to 1824 the Second Battalion was dissatisfied with its status in the Eleventh Regiment. The idea of forming a new regiment that would drill as infantry took hold and, despite numerous frustrations, would not die. The leaders in the movement were Major John D. Wilson, who had been Captain of the Fourth Company, Captain Prosper D. Wetmore, Brigade-Major, who had previously been Captain of the Third Company, and the four captains of the Second Battalion. During the winter and spring of 1824 they met regularly to discuss the project. Most of their time was spent in arguing over two problems. The first was the selection of a name for the new corps; the second was the design of a distinctive uniform.

The first problem was settled when the Marquis de Lafayette visited New York in the summer of 1824. New York's reception for the French hero was lavish and the Second Battalion took part in the military review held in his honor. While the troops were at the Battery awaiting the arrival of Lafayette, Major Wilson suddenly recalled the Marquis' connection with the famous National Guard of Paris. "Why not call our new corps the National Guards?" he exclaimed to the officers of the Second Battalion. The response was immediate and, at a meeting of the officers on August 25, was unanimously adopted. Lafayette was most grateful for the compliment. The following year, when he rode past the new battalion that bore the name of his beloved "National Guards," he stopped his carriage and insisted on shaking hands with each of the officers. The choice of a name was most propitious. As a symbol it immediately broadened the scope of the new corps and implied that it had a responsibility to the nation as well as to the city and state.

A happy accident settled the problem of choosing a uniform. On the morning of the parade for Lafayette, Sergeant Philetus D. Holt had left his blue artillery coat at the tailor's in Franklin Square. When he left his home he was dressed for the parade in the white trousers, white crossbelts, and plume of the Eleventh Regiment, and upon his shoulder he carried his musket. Holt was a flour merchant, and, over his uniform, he wore his business coat of gray cloth with metal buttons, and short skirts. On his way to the tailor he passed Prosper Wetmore's store in Pearl Street. Major Wilson happened to be there, and both of them were attracted by Holt's neat appearance in gray, gold, and white. Wilson was so delighted that he had a gray military coat made for himself and wore it to a meeting of the Battalion. Approval was unanimous and on August 30 the new uniform was adopted. The uniform "consisted of a short, single-breasted coat of cadet mixed cloth; square standing collar; three rows of buttons in front; black braid running back from each button across the breast; buttons and braid on the collar and cuffs; wings or shoulder-caps with black tufts; white trousers; glazed leather hat, with

bell crown, trimmed with gold and silver tassels; brass
initials 'N G' in cipher on front; white pompon; white
body-belt of webbing, with cartridge-box and bayonet-
sheath suspended therefrom; on the cartridge-box the cipher
'N G' in brass." [1]

A coat-of-arms was devised and designed by Sergeant
Asher Taylor of the Fourth Company. It consisted of a
shield quartered, showing: first, the shield of the United
States; second, the shield of the State of New York; third,
the shield of the City of New York; and fourth, the initials "N.Y.S.A." on a red ground, for the corps of
artillery.[2] At the base of the shield was the title, "National Guards." On the crest was an American eagle,
and the motto across the face, "Pro Patria et Gloria."
Taylor was a devoted member of the Seventh. He had
joined the Fourth Company in 1822, was a leader in the
movement to break away from the Eleventh Regiment, and
spent all his spare time until his death in 1878 in promoting
the interests of the Regiment.

In December 1824, the Fifth and Sixth Companies were
organized, and on June 27, 1825, Governor De Witt Clinton issued the order instituting the new Battalion of National Guards, thus achieving the separation from the
artillery battalion. The order, however, directed its con-
solidation with the infantry companies of the Second Regiment. The arrangement was a most unhappy one for those
who were seeking the establishment of a completely new
organization. Pressure was brought to bear therefore on the
Governor who issued a general order on October 1, 1825,
detaching the corps and organizing it into a separate battalion. The Seventh Company was organized in October
of that year; the Eighth on May 4, 1826. The battalion now
qualified for regimental status, and on May 6, 1826, the

Governor issued another order organizing the battalion into a regiment, to be named the Twenty-seventh Regiment of Artillery.

The new regiment had its growing pains during the first twenty years: from 1826 to 1847. It was not easy to come by a colonel who had the vision needed to mold this new corps into a crack regiment. Prosper M. Wetmore was a disappointment and resigned after one year, as a result of unfavorable publicity arising from his failure in business. Of the rest, during that period, only Linus W. Stevens made any significant contribution. In fact, it was his ability and spirit which kept the Regiment alive during those difficult times. It was a period of instability in New York and one of general apathy to all things military. The numerical strength of the Regiment never rose above 435 and was generally in the neighborhood of 370. Attendance at drill was hopelessly irregular. Furthermore, the regimental officers found it most difficult to instill in the members a sense of loyalty to the Regiment. The average member considered himself a First Company man, or a Fourth Company man, without feeling any sense of pride and loyalty to the Twenty-seventh. This would come eventually, but the progress was irritatingly slow.

One thing that helped was the startling discovery that the Regiment could be extraordinarily valuable in quelling local disorders. The elections in the spring of 1834 created a vast amount of excitement and hostility between the Whigs and the Democrats. At one point a riot broke out, when the Whigs seized the state arsenal. The police were helpless, and the Mayor found it necessary to call out the Twenty-seventh Regiment. Within two hours three hundred of its members were guarding the arsenal and patrolling the adjacent streets. This was a new and welcome development in the eyes of the civil authorities, and the Twenty-seventh was called out again in the Abolition Riot of 1834, the Stevedore Riot of 1836, the Flour Riot of 1837, and the Croton Water Works Riot of 1840.

The period of significant growth for the Regiment was ushered in by a major change in the militia laws of New York, which resulted in the renaming of the Twenty-seventh Regiment as the Seventh Regiment New York State Militia on July 27, 1847. During the 1840's the annual inspections showed a regimental strength of less than 400. Beginning in 1850 each year showed an annual increase in membership. By 1859 it had jumped to 910.

A major event in the history of the Seventh was the election of Abram Duryee as Colonel in 1849. His ten years in that office brought the Seventh to national renown, and much of the success was due to his efforts. Emmons Clark says of him:

> As commandant of the Seventh Regiment his military talents had wider scope, and secured universal appreciation and acknowledgment. To that high position he transferred the same talent, activity, energy, devotion, and enthusiasm which he had exhibited as a company officer, and he soon achieved the same success and distinction. Under his administration the Seventh Regiment acquired a higher reputation for the excellence of its drill, the completeness of its discipline, and the remarkable military pride and spirit of its members; and the distinguished services of Colonel Duryee, in securing this result, entitle him to rank among the most successful and accomplished militia officers that the United States has ever produced. He was an admirable instructor, and was cool, ready, and correct in his commands; his keen military eye and practical experience enabled him to detect and correct all errors; and he possessed a remarkable capacity for displaying the military

accomplishments of the Regiment, whenever occasion offered, to the best possible advantage.[3]

Abram Duryee was a highly successful mahogany merchant in New York, who had a positive passion for all things military. In 1833 at the age of eighteen he joined the 142d New York State Militia, but transferred to the First Company of the Twenty-seventh in 1838. One of his first jobs as Colonel was to lead his regiment in putting down the Astor Place Riots, which feat won so many friends for the Seventh. It also won for them the enmity of most of the less orderly elements of New York, and the nickname, "Old Greybacks."

Duryee had a genius for organization and a deep-seated conviction that the Seventh would become the Nation's number one civilian regiment. And, as the years went by, the dream began to come true. During the 1850's the enrollment jumped from 417 to 910. Tompkins Market was obtained as an armory, and for the first time the entire regiment was able to assemble under one roof. More important, the Seventh was acquiring a national reputation. Each year brought new calls upon the Regiment for attendance at ceremonies in all the large cities of the East and they were gradually being copied by other militia regiments. When Colonel Elmer Ellsworth brought his Chicago Zouaves to New York in 1860 he took note of this in a dinner speech:

> I resided in New York some five or six years ago, and often witnessed, with admiration and pride, the soldierly bearing and proficiency, in all martial exercises, of the Seventh Regiment; and afterward, in Chicago, when my comrades here did me the honor to call upon me to take command of them, I set before myself and them the

Seventh Regiment as our model—this is the secret of our success.[4]

In 1859 Colonel Duryee resigned his commission to the sincere regret of the entire Seventh. Others had been coming along, however, among them Marshall Lefferts who had joined the Regiment in 1851 and was elected lieutenant-colonel the following year. Lefferts was a distinguished professional engineer in New York and had an active part in the development of the telegraph industry. His election as Colonel in 1859 was universally approved and thus he became the Seventh's wartime commander.

And in the background during all these years was Asher Taylor, who always shunned honor but never varied in his devotion to the Seventh. Whether or not it was Taylor's idea to form a Veteran's Association cannot be verified. One thing can be certain: He was one of the principal instigators of the movement and its most ardent supporter. At any rate, on March 9, 1859, the Veterans of the National Guard was formed with John M. Catlin as Colonel, Linus W. Stevens, Lieutenant-Colonel, and James B. Wilson, Major. Its constitution stated its objects: 1. To constitute a bond of fellowship and union between former and present companions in arms; 2. To institute and perpetuate an official record and registry of the origin, acts, and members of the Seventh Regiment; and 3. To create a fund for useful and benevolent purposes.[5] The importance of this establishment may not have been fully recognized at the time. Eventually, however, it became a most essential bulwark of support for the Seventh Regiment and its most ardent champion.

III   Departure for Washington

In January 1861, the Regiment was well aware that their services might be needed by the Federal Government in the near future. The public mood of the North was indeed one of conciliation, born, however, not from affection for the South, but out of the union of discouragement and apathy. Mr. Buchanan was simply too timid and utterly incapable of providing the kind of presidential leadership needed in this crisis. For the blows were now falling down heavily on the hapless North. Mississippi rushed to follow South Carolina out of the Union; then Florida and Alabama, with Georgia, Louisiana, and Texas on their heels. They seized United States property within their borders, but the Government made no effort to reclaim it. It was becoming increasingly difficult to appease the South and thoughtful men were aware that the conciliatory mood was fast petering out and would change with the new Administration. Down in Washington, General Scott had already talked about the possibility of using the Seventh Regiment. On the eighth of January rumors broke out that a Virginian mob was about to attack the city, and many families were leaving for Philadelphia and New York. Scott, however, felt that he could handle the situation with several companies of

regular troops scheduled to arrive and the District militia.
Besides, as he pointed out to Senator LaFayette S. Foster of
Connecticut, if more men were wanted, "I shall write to
my friend General Sandford of New York, who has con-
siderable military capacity, and request him to send me the
Seventh Regiment. That regiment, Sir, can be relied upon.
It will stand being brick-batted without drawing a trigger
till it is ordered to fire!" [1]

Despite strong opposition to the incoming Republican
Administration from sizable factions in New York, there
was genuine public anger as news came in during January
of states seceding and the seizure of government forts,
arsenals, and other property. The excitement was particularly high on January 9 when the *Star of the West*, which
had been despatched from New York City with supplies
for Fort Sumter, was fired upon in Charleston Harbor.
This was the signal for Republican action and the Legislature immediately adopted a joint resolution, with only
three dissenting votes. The action cited the insurrection in
South Carolina and the seizure of government property
there and in three other Southern states; took note of the
treasonable acts of United States Senators; tendered to the
President "whatever aid in men and money may be required to enable him to enforce the laws and uphold the
authority of the Federal Government." [2]

In this atmosphere the Board of Officers of the Seventh
Regiment met on January 14 to discuss the situation. At
this meeting Major Alexander Shaler introduced the following resolution, which was adopted:

> Resolved, That, should the exigency arise, we feel con-
> fident in having the commandant express to the Governor
> of the State the desire of this regiment to perform such
> duty as he may prescribe.[3]

It is probable that notice of this action was sent directly to General Scott, although General Charles W. Sandford, as Commander of the First Division of New York State Militia, must have received the communication officially. At any rate, Sandford, who was at this time busy planning for the possible federalization of his command, was able to inform Scott on the sixteenth:

> Being under the impression that the state of the country might render it necessary to withdraw for service elsewhere the whole or a large part of the troops now occupying posts in the harbor of New York, I take great pleasure in saying, with the approval of Governor Morgan, with whom I have conferred on this subject, that I can furnish from the First Division New York State Militia, at any time, a sufficient force to take charge of the fortifications in our harbor as long as may be necessary. And should it be necessary (as I trust it will not) to sustain the Government and keep the peace at Washington by a larger force than you can concentrate from the U.S. Army, I can send you, at short notice, five or six good regiments, upon which you could rely with confidence.[4]

This was not yet the time to bring outside troops into Washington, however, and General Scott turned down the offer on January 17 in a letter to Governor E. D. Morgan, of New York:

> I am very sure that the President, as yet, has not seriously thought of calling for volunteers or militia from any quarter beyond this District; and to maintain the peace here the local militia, the constabulary, and some 700 regulars, including three companies of horse or flying artillery, are at present deemed sufficient.

Perhaps no regiment or company can be brought here from a distance without producing hurtful jealousies in this vicinity.

If there be an exception, it is the Seventh Infantry, of the city of New York, which has become somewhat national, and it is held deservedly in the highest respect from its escorting the remains of President Monroe from New York to Richmond, and its presence at the inauguration of the statue of the Father of his Country in Washington.[5]

Two weeks later came another false start. The electoral votes for President were to be counted on February 13 and the War Department became increasingly nervous as they contemplated the possible disorders that might occur. Although the correspondence is lacking, the Seventh Regiment must have been in the minds of Washington officials, for General Sandford secretly called together the field officers and company commanders of the Regiment on February 8. At that meeting he informed them that Governor Morgan had been notified that he would probably be called upon for eight hundred militia to repair to Washington, and to be present at the Capitol on the Thirteenth of February. Following this conference the officers were all summoned to meet on February 10 to receive orders for the Regiment to proceed to Washington. Scott, however, still felt that he could handle the situation with his available forces, and the Board of Officers received the following note from General Sandford:

No. 312 West 22d Street.
New York, February 10, 1861.

My Dear Colonel: I am happy to inform you that there will be no immediate occasion for our services.

Be pleased to return my thanks to your officers for their attendance, and continue the injunction of silence.

I am Very Truly
Your Ob'dt Serv'nt,
Charles W. Sandford.[6]

Col. Marshall Lefferts
7th Reg't.

The fall of Sumter, of course, removed all uncertainty, and the involvement of the Regiment began as soon as Lincoln's proclamation calling for troops was announced on April 15. In Albany the legislature was in session, due to adjourn on the following day. Governor Morgan accordingly acted immediately and sent a message to the Assembly:

> . . . It is not doubted that New York will be at once called upon for a large quota of militia. It would seem therefore most clearly to be the part of wisdom, no less than the dictate of patriotism, that a military force be authorized sufficiently large to meet the present and prospective demands of the General Government; and to place such force at the disposal of the Federal authorities. I would, therefore, respectfully, though earnestly, urge that the Legislature, without delay, confer larger discretionary power than is now possessed to embody and equip a volunteer militia for the public defence, and to provide the necessary means therefor.[7]

Within a few hours the legislature had passed a bill establishing a State Military Board, composed of the Governor, the Lieutenant-Governor, the Secretary of State, the Comptroller, the State Engineer and Surveyor, and the State Treasurer. The board was empowered to accept into the service of the state, in addition to and as a part of its militia, thirty thousand volunteers for two years.

In New York City Colonel Lefferts was equally prompt as soon as he heard of the President's proclamation. Under the authority granted him by the officers' resolution of January 14, he notified Governor Morgan that his regiment was available for service and then called a meeting of the Board of Officers for the following day. At this meeting on April 16 forty officers were present and unanimously adopted the following resolution:

> Resolved: That the Colonel be requested to notify the Major-General that this Regiment responds to the call of the country as made by the President through the Governor of the State, and that the Regiment is ready to march forthwith.[8]

Governor Morgan now had to decide how best to carry out the President's call for seventeen regiments from New York State. For this purpose he met with his newly created military board on the evening of April 16. The Governor submitted a dispatch from Simon Cameron, the Secretary of War, demanding, "that the men called for were to be mustered into immediate service and that he would be gratified to have one or more regiments march to Washington before the close of the week." [9] This presented some knotty problems to the Board. In the first place only two of the volunteer militia organizations were fully equipped, uniformed, and ready to march, the Fifth and the Seventh Infantry. The remaining units generally were badly equipped and insufficiently uniformed. The Sixty-ninth Infantry, for example, had only 380 men uniformed out of 1050.[10] Obviously, in the emergency the board would have to overlook this situation, but it was a factor in the discussion. In the second place, it was going to be difficult to order such a considerable number of men, many of them importantly

engaged in industry, commerce, and the professions to drop
everything at short notice and march off to Washington.
The best solution seemed to be the recruitment of 17 new
volunteer regiments of 780 men each. The term of enlistment was to be for two years. The Board thereupon adopted
a resolution to that effect. In order to meet the immediate
demand for the relief of Washington, the existing volunteer militia regiments were to be ordered out as quickly as
possible, to serve until they were relieved by the new regiments. Colonel Lefferts' offer had come at the right time,
and the Governor that evening decided to order the Seventh Regiment to Washington.[11] The actual orders were
to be issued the following day, and Governor Morgan so
records the date in the Minutes of his Military Board of
April 22, 1861:

> As a matter of information the Governor reported that
> on the 17th instant he ordered 7th Regiment to proceed
> to Washington, in conformity with the Requisition of the
> President, and report to the President of the United
> States.[12]

The next day Tompkins Market Armory came to life as
the news of the departure of the Regiment spread throughout the city. Members of the Regiment bustled about
everywhere, buttonholing each other for the latest scrap of
news. Adding to the excitement was the appearance of so
many ex-members of the Regiment who begged to rejoin.
These and a host of new applicants besieged Colonel
Lefferts at his regimental office and at his home during the
evening of the seventeenth and throughout the next two
days. Since regimental standards were so high, most of these
applicants had to be turned away, although the best of
them were accepted. Among those admitted at this time

was Schuyler Hamilton who had been on the staff of General Scott during the Mexican War. Generally, however, it was essential to hold down the size of the Regiment to manageable limits. As it was, the regimental roster had shown an active strength of 895 men on January 1, 1861,[13] which increased to 991 on April 19.

The main concern of Colonel Lefferts and his officers on the seventeenth, however, was to make sure that nothing interfered with the immediate issuance of orders for the Regiment to march. General Sandford also appears to have been anxious for his "crack" regiment to be among the first to go to the relief of Washington. For, as soon as he was notified of the action of the Board of Officers, he not only notified the Governor but also telegraphed to General Scott that "the Seventh Regiment was ready and waiting orders to proceed to Washington." [14] Lefferts, however, was taking no chances that Scott might misunderstand their state of readiness and followed up with another telegram:

New York, 17th April, 1861.
Lieutenant-General Winfield Scott, U.S.A.

Sir,—Major-General Sandford **has already telegraphed** and written, informing you that the Seventh Regiment New York State Militia are ready, and waiting orders, to proceed to Washington as per order of the Governor. I fear that he may have failed to inform you that we have a full set of camp equipage, and can and should prefer to go into camp within the vicinity of Washington; but of course have no preference over your orders.

I have the honor to remain,
Your obedient servant,
Marshall Lefferts,
Colonel Commanding[15]

Scott scarcely needed convincing. He was familiar with the Regiment and admired it as a well-trained and disciplined unit. Concern over the danger to Washington was mounting hourly and the General knew he could count on the Seventh to respond quickly. Besides, the Regiment had a national reputation and the news of its muster into federal service would be a splendid morale booster. Thus, he replied immediately to Sandford:

> War Department
> Washington City, April 17, 1861
>
> Maj. Gen. C. W. Sandford,
> 　New York City:
> 　Send to this place the Seventh Regiment by rail. See quartermaster, No. 6 State street, for transportation, and telegraph me the hour of departure from New York.
>
> Winfield Scott[16]

Meanwhile, despite its plentiful equipment, the Regiment was badly in need of funds for the campaign. Food and other supplies would have to be procured; additional ammunition might have to be purchased. The state was expected to provide for its troops until they were mustered into Federal service, but the need was immediate. In the emergency, then, the merchants of New York came to the rescue. Meeting in the Chamber of Commerce on Wednesday, April 17, thirty-one gentlemen immediately gave a hundred dollars each "for the equipment of the Seventh Regiment for active service." Before the meeting was over the list of donors was doubled, and a total sum of $6,140 collected. The following were the subscribers at this time:

$100.00 SUBSCRIPTIONS

Moses H. Grinnell　　　　　Moses Taylor
George B. DeForrest　　　　Theodore Dehon

L. G. Cannon
C. R. Robert
Royal Phelps
S. Wetmore
R. M. Blatchford
Thomas Addis Emmet
A. C. Gray
W. B. Duncan
Phelps, Dodge, & Co.
Charles H. Russell
Edwin Bartlett
Charles Christmas
Edward Minturn
S. B. Chittenden
A. V. Stout
W. Whitewright, Jr.
John L. Aspinwall
J. F. D. Lanier
Henry Chauncey
August Belmont
Clark & Mosely
Benj. Nathan
W. W. De Forest
Isaac Bell
Howell L. Williams
Almon W. Griswold
Bleeker Outhout
R. Alsop

Ogden Haggerty
William M. Evarts
G. S. Robbins
George Griswold
John A. Stevens
James Gallatin
E. Walker & Son
H. R. Dunham
Hamilton Fish
Robert B. Minturn
D. F. Manice
James H. Titus
William Curtis Noyes
Charles H. Marshall
Stewart Brown
Andrew Foster
Joseph W. Alsop
Joseph Gaillard, Jr.
James S. Wadsworth
John Bridge
Benj. F. Breeden
P. S. Forbes
Charles Davis
Frederick Bronson
B. H. Hutton
Aymar & Co.
Levi E. Morton
Benj. L. Swan

$50.00 SUBSCRIPTIONS

George W. Blunt
G. C. Ward

Henry Chauncey, Jr.

$25.00 SUBSCRIPTIONS

C. B. Loomis

$20.00 SUBSCRIPTIONS

Rufus Prime   Washington Coster

In addition, the New York Stock Exchange contributed a thousand dollars at this meeting.

By evening of the seventeenth the orders to march had not yet been received, and the left-wing drill, which had been previously scheduled, was held before a larger-than-usual throng of spectators. The Regiment had become so large during the last year that drills had to be held in sections because the Armory was not large enough. During the exercise General Sandford arrived at the Armory and informed Colonel Lefferts of the telegram from General Scott. He also had with him orders for the Regiment from Albany. Immediately after the drill the Board of Officers was called together and General Sandford announced that

> the Seventh Regiment was honored by being the *first* called into the service of the country. The time of leaving New York for Washington was a subject of considerable discussion, but it was decided that the Regiment would take a much larger number of its members if its departure was delayed until Friday, the 19th, and the division order was issued accordingly. . . . In reply to a question as to how long the Regiment would be detained at Washington, General Sandford stated that the time would probably be from two to four weeks, and that it would certainly be relieved within that period by other troops, to be enlisted especially for the United States service.[17]

The following orders were thereupon published and distributed to the Regiment about midnight on the seventeenth.

General Head-Quarters, State of New York
Adjutant-General's Office, Albany,
April 17, 1861

General Orders No. 43

In pursuance of a requisition from the President of the United States, Major-General Sandford is hereby directed to detail one regiment of 800 men, or two regiments amounting to the same number, for immediate service, to be reported forthwith to the President of the United States, to serve until relieved by other regiments, or by a regiment or regiments of Volunteer Militia, to be organized under an Act of the Legislature of the State, passed April 16, 1861.

By order of the Commander-in-Chief:
J. Meredith Read, Jr., Adjutant-General

With these, came Sandford's special orders for the movement of the Regiment:

Head Quarters, First Division, N.Y.S.M.
New York, April 17, 1861.

Special Order No. 8

In pursuance of the foregoing general orders No. 43, from General Head-quarters, the Seventh Regiment N.Y.S.M., under the command of Colonel Lefferts, is hereby detailed for immediate service at the national capital.

Colonel Lefferts will direct his Quartermaster to report, at noon tomorrow, to the Major-General, for orders for the transportation of the regiment, its camp equipage and baggage, and for a requisition for a sufficient quantity of ammunition to furnish each man with twenty-four rounds.

Colonel Lefferts will order his regiment to assemble at their armory on Friday next, at 3 o'clock, P.M., armed and equipped for embarkation, each man supplied with provisions for twenty-four hours.

Colonel Lefferts, upon his arrival at Washington, will report for orders to Lieutenant-General Scott.

The Major-General congratulates the Seventh Regiment upon being the first corps detailed from this State, in response to the call of the constituted authorities of our country, to support the Union and the Constitution, and to vindicate the honor of that glorious flag which was consecrated by the blood of our fathers.

Brigadier-General Hall will promulgate this order immediately.

By order of
Charles W. Sandford
Major-General Commanding[18]

Although these orders are dated April 17, there is a strong possibility that the exact time for the Regiment to assemble at the Armory was not inserted until the following day. For it was not until the morning of April 18 that Colonel Lefferts was informed by the United States Quartermaster-General that he would be unable to furnish transportation for an earlier hour than five P.M. of the following day, the nineteenth. As to ammunition, Sandford explained his action to Governor Morgan in the postscript of a letter dated April 19, 1861.

P.S. As there were hostile indications in Maryland, I deemed it necessary to issue ball cartridges for the Troops sent, & have made requisitions on Cm. Genl. Welsh which have been promptly responded to. I have also authorized the 7th to take their howitzers & ammunitions. All of which I trust you will approve.

C.W.S.[19]

April 18 brought a new frenzy of war fervor to New York when the morning newspapers announced that the Seventh was leaving for Washington. To add to the excitement, the

Sixth Massachusetts Regiment arrived early in the morning and breakfasted at the Astor House. They then marched down Broadway and left Jersey City at eleven A.M. Meantime, into New York Harbor came the U.S.S. *Baltic* carrying Major Anderson and his entire command from Fort Sumter. Thus the city forgot all about business for the day and gave itself over to the excitement.

At the Armory the entire Seventh Regiment assembled for a mass-meeting during the morning, at which the speeches of the Colonel and the other officers were received with wild enthusiasm. At this time the regimental orders were issued:

Head-quarters, Seventh Regiment, N.Y.S.M.
New York, April 18, 1861.

General Orders No. 5

In compliance with orders from his Excellency the Governor, and division orders of this date, this regiment will assemble at Head-quarters on Friday, 19th instant, at three o'clock, P.M., in full fatigue and overcoat, with knapsack, to embark for Washington City.

The men will each take one blanket, to be rolled on top of knapsack, suitable underclothing, an extra pair of boots (shoes are better), knife, fork, spoon, tin cup, plate, body-belt, and cap-pouch, to be carried in the knapsack. The men will provide themselves with one day's rations.

There will be allowed three servants to each company, who must report to the Quartermaster at twelve o'clock, M., and receive their "pass." Each officer will be allowed one small trunk, which must be distinctly marked and left at the armory before twelve M., 19th instant.

All uniformed men, whether recruits or not, will report for duty. Recruits who have just joined will also report, and will be assigned a post in column.

Commissary Patten will receive instructions from the
Colonel, and leave for Washington this P.M.

Appointments.—J. C. Dalton, Jr., M.D., Surgeon's Mate,
vice Cameron, resigned.

By order of
Marshall Lefferts, Colonel [20]
J. H. Liebenau, Adjutant

Appended to the orders was a notice requesting the hon-
orary members of the Regiment and those excused from
duty for various reasons to send overcoats and knapsacks
to the Armory immediately for the use of the new recruits.

As one of the final pieces of business, arrangements had
to be made for the care of the Armory during the absence
of the Regiment. This task was to be assigned to the
Veterans of the Seventh Regiment, an organization which
had been formed in 1859. Accordingly, Asher Taylor,
Adjutant of the Veterans, issued a call for a meeting on the
evening of April 18. There, Colonel Lefferts expressed the
Regiment's gratitude to the Veterans for their offer and
formally placed the custody of the Armory in their hands.
A uniformed battalion of the Organization was then formed,
which stayed in existence until 1892.

The nineteenth of April was the anniversary of the Battle
of Lexington, and, appropriately enough, the Eighth Massachusetts Regiment, like revified Minutemen, arrived in
town early in the morning. They were accompanied by
Benjamin F. Butler, who was Brigadier-General of all Massachusetts troops. As on the previous day, the Astor House
extended its hospitality and the Regiment breakfasted there,
while Butler and his staff went off to the Fifth Avenue
Hotel. By this time, the city was beginning to stir, and
huge numbers of people began pouring out into the streets.
It was evident that New York, which never did anything

by halves, was going to outdo itself in sending the regiments
off to war. Thus, the Eighth Massachusetts found itself
marching down a Broadway packed with cheering onlookers,
on their way to the Jersey City Ferry, where they departed
at eleven A.M.

The heart of New York, however, was over in Tompkins
Square where its own Seventh Regiment was getting ready.
New York had always fussed over and pampered the
Seventh. It was proud that the Regiment was considered
the crack militia unit of the Nation; it liked to boast of the
honors and tributes that kept coming in from all parts of
the country during the past few years. Today its "darling"
was going off to war, and it was only proper that the send-
off should break all records. Thus, long before noon the
crowds were out in the streets and the flags began to appear. As *The New York Times* recounted it:

> The Stars and Stripes were everywhere, from the cost-
> liest silk, twenty, thirty, forty feet in length to the home-
> lier bunting, down to the few inches of painted calico that
> a baby's hand might wave. It would be invidious to say
> from what buildings the National flag was displayed, be-
> cause it would be almost impossible to tell from what
> buildings it did not wave, and never, if flags can be ani-
> mated with any of the feelings of their owners, with a
> purer devotion to the Union. Evidently, all political par-
> tisanship was cast aside. But the gayest, and in this respect,
> the most remarkable thoroughfare was Cortlandt Street.
> Lafayette Place where the Regiment was to form previous
> to marching was very attractively dressed—a huge flag
> being displayed from the Astor Library, among numerous
> others from private buildings. But Cortlandt Street showed
> a gathering of flags, a perfect army of them. They were not
> in that comparatively brief space from Broadway to the
> Jersey City ferry, to be numbered by dozens or by scores;

every building seemed like "Captains of Fifties." It was flag, flag, from every window from the first floor to the roof,—in short it was flag, flag,—and of quite large sizes too till the wearied eye refused the task of counting them. Such was the display along the route of the Seventh.[21]

Fitz-James O'Brien was a private in Company G. He was also a well-known and accomplished journalist, who has left a delightful account of the Regiment's march to Washington. As he recalls the morning of the nineteenth:

All day long, from an early hour in the morning, young men in uniforms or civilian's dress, might have been seen hurrying up and down Broadway, with anomalous-looking bundles under their arms. Dandies, who were the pride of club windows, were not above brown paper parcels; military tailors were stormed and taken with considerable loss —to the pocket. Delmonico, calm and serene, superintended sandwiches which were destined for the canteen. People in the streets looked with a sort of regretful admiration at the gray uniforms hurrying by. Hardware stores were ransacked of revolvers. A feverish excitement throbbed through the city—the beating of that big Northern pulse, so slow, so sure, and so steady.[22]

About noon, the members of the Regiment began to arrive at the Armory, most of them in carriages accompanied by their families. Inside, all was confusion, as the drill halls and the company rooms began to fill up. The officers were particularly hard-pressed. Colonel Lefferts found himself without a lieutenant-colonel, as the report came in that W. A. Pond was too ill to accompany the Regiment. The First, Seventh, Ninth, and Tenth companies were without captains. Nevertheless, some semblance of order began to emerge as the time for muster drew near. Lefferts spent a good part of his time receiving visitors

who overwhelmed him with generous offers of aid to the
Regiment. Also, he still had to fend off late applicants who
wanted to join up at the last minute. Edward Minturn, who
had been the leader in the Chamber of Commerce fund-
raising two days before, was on hand with news of more
gifts. As part of the fund, Lefferts received that morning the
sum of one thousand dollars to "do what he pleased with
for the comfort of the regiment." Part of this he used to
buy revolvers for his officers, and the rest was turned over
to the regimental fund. Another visitor was E. H. Simon,
Esq., of the Seventy-first Militia, who presented a national
flag. Among others, was the director of one of the insurance
companies, who appeared before the Fifth company to
pledge an annuity of a thousand dollars for the wife of one
of its members, if he should be killed in battle.

In the middle of the commotion a telegram arrived from
S. M. Felton, president of the Philadelphia, Wilmington,
and Baltimore Railroad: "Don't let this by any means get
into the newspapers. Make your arrangements to leave New
York as many hours earlier than five o'clock as you possibly
can." [23] Felton was probably aware at this point of trouble
in Baltimore, for soon after, at about three P.M. the startling news came that the Sixth Massachusetts had been
attacked by a mob in Baltimore, with some casualties, and
had to fight its way through the city. Lefferts now had to
consider the possibility that his own passage through Baltimore might be disputed, or that he might have to find some
way to avoid the city. At this point he was probably thank-
ful that Sandford had decided to issue ammunition to his
command.

At three P.M. the drums began to roll and each company
assembled in its own room. The orderlies read the rolls; the
company commanders issued last minute instructions; and

finally the men were marched into position in the large hall and drill room. Outside, the crowd had now become so dense that the police had difficulty in opening a narrow lane into the Armory. They cheered wildly as a huge van drawn by eight horses pulled away with the officers' baggage. And in the Ninth Company, Pvt. Theodore Winthrop, who was assigned to take care of the two little brass howitzers, moved them with his crew down the rear stairs. They then stationed them in back of the building and spent the next hour trying to keep the crowds away from the guns.

The Regiment moved out into Lafayette Place at four P.M. and lined up between Fourth and Eighth streets. Some of the men had not yet arrived and, at this point, there were 945 in line. By the time the Regiment left Jersey City, however, the number had increased to 991. After a half-hour of sergeants' reports and reassignments to equalize the companies, the police platoons opened the way through the crowds, "the band burst out with martial music, the howitzers rattled forward, drawn by the men assigned to them, the companies wheeled into column, and, amid a fresh outburst of cheers and songs and fresh tears and farewell gestures from the overlooking windows, the regiment moved along Lafayette Place, bowered in flags and streamers, turned into Great Jones Street and thence into Broadway." [24] At the head of the column was an impromptu escort of Zouaves with "red shirts, blue flowing trousers, gay fez caps, and hairy knapsacks trussed up behind."

By now almost the entire city had turned out and the Regiment had great difficulty making its way through the dense crowds. At the corner of Prince Street Major Anderson stood on the balcony of Ball, Black, and Company and reviewed the Regiment as it passed. At one point the crowd got between the band and the companies and had to be cleared at bayonet point. Private Winthrop, marching along with his howitzers, has left a vivid description of the march:

At a great house on the left, as we pass the Astor Library, I see a handkerchief waving for me. Yes! it is she who made the sandwiches in my knapsack. They were a trifle too thick, as I afterwards discovered, but otherwise perfection. Be these my thanks and the thanks of hungry comrades who had bites of them!

At the corner of Great Jones Street we halted for half an hour—then, everything ready, we marched down Broadway.

It was worth a life, that march. Only one who passed, as we did, through that tempest of cheers, two miles long, can know the terrible enthusiasm of the occasion. I could hardly hear the rattle of our own gun-carriages, and only once or twice the music of our band came to me muffled and quelled by the uproar. We knew now, if we had not before divined it, that our great city was with us as one man, utterly united in the great cause we were marching to sustain.

This grand fact I learned by two senses. If hundreds of thousands roared it into my ears, thousands slapped it into my back. My fellow-citizens smote me on the knapsack, as I went by at the gun rope, and encouraged me each in his own dialect. "Bully for you!" alternated with benedictions, in the proportion of two "bullies" to one blessing.

I was not so fortunate as to receive more substantial tokens of sympathy. But there were parting gifts showered on the regiment, enough to establish a variety shop. Handkerchiefs, of course, came floating down upon us from the windows, like snow. Pretty little gloves pelted us with love-taps. The sterner sex forced upon us pocket-knives new and jagged, combs, soap, slippers, boxes of matches, cigars by the dozen and the hundred, pipes to smoke shag and pipes to smoke Latakia, fruit, eggs, and sandwiches. One fellow got a new purse with ten bright quarter-eagles.[25]

Finally the Regiment turned down Cortlandt Street from Broadway at about 5:30 P.M. and managed to push its way through the heaviest jam of all in the ferry square. There the boats were waiting for them, and, with all the ships in the harbor decorated with flags and pennants, the Regiment left New York and landed in Jersey City.

IV Philadelphia and the Chesapeake

ANY THOUGHT that the Regiment could slip through New Jersey quietly and quickly was dispelled when the ferry boats reached Jersey City. The huge depot of the New Jersey Railroad was so crowded that the Regiment had difficulty in pushing its way through to the train awaiting them. Eventually, however, the troops and *impedimenta* were loaded and the long train pulled out at 6:40 P.M. The progress through New Jersey was unbelievably slow, because at every station huge crowds had turned out to greet the Regiment. According to Fitz-James O'Brien,

> All along the track shouting crowds, hoarse and valorous, sent to us, as we passed, their hopes and wishes. When we stopped at the different stations, rough hands came in through the windows, apparently unconnected with any one in particular until you shook them, and then the subtle magnetic thrill told that there were bold hearts beating at the end. This continued until night closed, and, indeed, until after midnight.[1]

Equally impressed, Winthrop adds that, "I think I did not see a rod of ground without its man, from dusk till dawn, from the Hudson to the Delaware." [2]

At some time between one-thirty and two A.M. the train

arrived at Camden where the Regiment was ferried across the Delaware to Philadelphia. They then marched up Washington Street to the Broad Street Depot of the Philadelphia, Wilmington, and Baltimore Railroad, where they boarded the Baltimore cars and settled down to wait for the next move.[3] In his official report Colonel Lefferts notes the time of arrival in Philadelphia as three-thirty A.M. on April 20.[4]

At this point any expectation of being able to leave Philadelphia quickly was dimmed immediately by the muddled situation that existed there. The riot in Baltimore on the nineteenth, in which the Sixth Massachusetts had to fight its way through the city, proved more serious than at first imagined. During the day it had become evident to Samuel M. Felton, president of the Philadelphia, Wilmington and Baltimore Railroad, and J. Edgar Thomson, President of the Pennsylvania Railroad, that they faced a formidable problem in transporting troops from Philadelphia to Washington. There was no difficulty on the line from Philadelphia to Perryville, on the east bank of the Susquehanna River. In 1861 the river had not yet been bridged, and passengers for Baltimore had to transfer to a ferryboat, cross the river, and board other cars at Havre de Grace. From that place to Washington trouble could be anticipated, particularly if the rioting spread beyond Baltimore. There was a good possibility that the rebels would disrupt railroad communication between Havre de Grace and Baltimore by destroying the bridges over Bush River and Gunpowder River.

Felton and Thomson had lost no time in reporting the situation to the Secretary of War. As soon as the report came in of the riot, they telegraphed Cameron:

We are informed here that the troops sent last night have been stopped at Baltimore, and that it is impracticable to send more through that city. Shall we send them by steamer to Annapolis? [5]

This would be an excellent solution, and fairly obvious. Washington was only thirty miles from Annapolis. If troops could be landed there, they could either march over the wagon road to the Capital, or use the branch railroad that ran from Annapolis to Annapolis Junction, where they could be shifted to the main line into Washington. It was most likely that the government would have little difficulty in retaining control of the railroad as far as Annapolis Junction.

When Cameron did not answer, the two railroad men sent him another telegram:

Having arrived at Philadelphia, we are informed by the Baltimore road that Governor Hicks states that no troops can pass through Baltimore City; in fact the Baltimore and Ohio Railroad refuse to transfer. We will wait for instructions.[6]

Some time later, probably late in the evening of the nineteenth, an answer came signed by L. Thomas, Adjutant-General,

Governor Hicks has neither right nor authority to stop troops coming to Washington.

Send them on prepared to fight their way through, if necessary.

By order of the Secretary of War.

Why Cameron should have sent this type of military order to Felton and Thomson is difficult to understand. Evidently communication between the Secretary and his commanding general must have been scanty, for Scott had, on that day, placed Robert Patterson in command of the Military Department of Washington, which was extended to include Delaware and Pennsylvania, as well as the District of Columbia and Maryland. Patterson was the Major-General in command of Pennsylvania volunteers. He was then sixty-eight years old and had served with distinction in the Mexican War. However, as shown later in the Bull Run disaster, he was not quite up to the task of taking hold of a situation quickly. Thus, both General Butler who arrived with the Eighth Massachusetts at four P.M., and, later, Lefferts with his Seventh New York found themselves operating almost independently of the actual military commander of the area.

During the evening of the nineteenth, Felton, Thomson, the Governor of Pennsylvania, and the Mayor of Philadelphia met with General Patterson at his home. Apparently no word had come as yet from the Secretary of War in reply to the earlier telegrams. The discussion, therefore, centered around the alternate route through Annapolis. Even when Cameron's reply was received, no one had any qualms about ignoring it, for it would have been foolhardy to send raw militia troops through hostile territory with insufficient ammunition. By this time Felton and Thomson had received reports that the bridges on the line between Havre de Grace and Baltimore had been, or were about to be, burned. Actually, according to the later report of George W. Brown, Mayor of Baltimore, he ordered them to be burned about midnight on the nineteenth, with the acquiescence of Governor Hicks of Maryland. Under these circumstances all agreed on the desirability of the Annapolis route, and Felton was asked to call on General Butler, who had arrived earlier.

Butler, with his staff, was at the Continental Hotel, and Felton, accompanied by Captain (later Admiral) Samuel F. DuPont, Commander of the Philadelphia Navy Yard, met him there. They informed him that General Patterson "most urgently advised that he should go to Annapolis." [7] This did not go over well with the Massachusetts general, who felt that Patterson, as a major-general, should issue him orders instead of advice. Butler's thinking, at least as expressed later in his memoirs, was that under the Articles of War the senior officer present should take command when two or more units of troops were at the same location.[8] The principal difficulty with this method of reasoning was that neither the Eighth Massachusetts, nor the Seventh New York, had as yet been mustered into federal service. They were, therefore, still under the orders of the governors of their respective states. They could with justification disregard orders from higher ranking officers on the way to Washington, unless specific instructions came directly from the Secretary of War or General Scott. This was probably in Patterson's mind on the nineteenth when he attempted to use persuasion instead of command.

Convincing Butler that he should proceed to Annapolis was no easy task. Felton put the ferryboat *Maryland*, which was at Perryville, at the disposal of the Massachusetts regiment. They could thus sail down Chesapeake Bay and land at Annapolis. Butler, whose account of this meeting seems slightly confused, suggested the possibility that the *Maryland* might have been seized by the rebels, or would be before he could get there. To this DuPont answered that it was also possible to obtain a vessel at Philadelphia and sail directly to Annapolis. Butler then came up with a rather vague plan of joining with Lefferts' Seventh New York and proceeding together to Washington. Precisely what he had in mind is difficult to determine from his memoirs. In his dispatch to Governor Andrew he talks about proceeding with the fifteen hundred troops "in marching order from Havre de Grace to Washington." In the next sentence, however, he proposes to take the troops to Annapolis, arriving there about four o'clock. This must mean that he intended to load both regiments on the *Maryland*, since an overland march could not possibly be accomplished in such a short time. It should have been obvious to him, however, that the ferryboat was not large enough to accommodate both regiments. At least two trips would have to be made, forcing an intolerable delay. At any rate it appears that no decision was made at the meeting. According to Butler's account, he intended to ask Lefferts to march with him. If Lefferts refused, he proposed to take his regiment to Perryville and sail on the *Maryland* to Annapolis.[9]

After leaving Butler, Felton went to the Broad Street depot to meet Lefferts. By this time he had telegraphic communication that the bridges between Havre de Grace and Baltimore were being destroyed. He also had communications from Governor Hicks and Mayor Brown forbidding the passage of troops through Baltimore. Lefferts immediately called his officers into Felton's office for consultation. From General Patterson's advice and Felton's information it was immediately apparent that the original plan of moving through Baltimore would have to be abandoned. With railroad communication cut, this would mean an eighty mile march from Havre de Grace to Washington with inadequate provisions, ammunition, and hospital supplies, an almost impossible task for a regiment fresh from civilian life. More important still, it might lead to considerable delay in relieving Washington, and the

Seventh was under strict orders to report to the President as quickly as possible.

Three other possible routes presented themselves. The Regiment could move by rail to Perryville, and thence to Annapolis on the *Maryland.* This plan had two drawbacks. It was quite conceivable that the rebels might capture and destroy the *Maryland,* which would mean bringing the entire regiment back to Philadelphia and starting over again. Besides, the Eighth Massachusetts also needed transportation, which brought up gloomy visions of the ferryboat shuttling back and forth, while parts of the regiments waited at Perryville. A second possibility was to charter a steamer at Philadelphia. The route to Washington would be down Delaware Bay into the Atlantic Ocean, thence up Chesapeake Bay and the Potomac River. This would be the quickest route, but risky, if no convoy were available to take the unarmed vessel up the possibly hostile river. The final choice was to sail directly from Philadelphia to Annapolis, which meant going all the way around Cape Charles and up Chesapeake Bay, a voyage of approximately 350 miles.

Judging from Colonel Lefferts' telegrams to the Secretary of War on the morning of the twentieth, the decision of the officers appears to have been in favor of proceeding to Annapolis by way of Perryville. It had been planned to bring the Regiment through Baltimore, and Lefferts decided, quite properly, that he should try to get authorization for a change in route. Therefore, unlike Butler who should have done the same, he sent the following telegram:

Philadelphia, 5 o'clock A.M.
April 20, 1861

Hon. S. Cameron, Secretary of War, Washington.

Sir,—Having arrived at Philadelphia, we are informed

by the President of the Philadelphia and Baltimore Railroad that Governor Hicks states that no more troops can pass. In fact, the Baltimore and Ohio Road refuses to transport. We will wait for instructions.

Marshall Lefferts[10]

When no answer came back, he concluded that the telegraph lines were down, but decided to send another message. This time he was more specific.

Philadelphia, Pa., April 20, 1861

Hon. Simon Cameron, Secretary of War:

Will you give order to dispatch troops via Annapolis today from here to Havre de Grace by rail, thence by large iron ferry-boat? The Baltimore and Ohio Road decline to transport any more troops from the North. We think this decidedly best, and are joined in this opinion by General Patterson, General Cadwalader, and Governor Curtin.

M. Lefferts,
Colonel Seventh N.Y.S.M.[11]

It is most difficult to determine at what point Colonel Lefferts and his officers decided to abandon the Perryville route and charter a vessel at Philadelphia. From the above telegram it is evident that they had come to a decision, but the likelihood is that the idea of sailing from Philadelphia had been under constant discussion during the night. Time passed on, however, and no reply came from the Secretary of War. At seven A.M. General Butler appeared at the depot in search of Colonel Lefferts. The interview was somewhat less than cordial. Butler seems to have been keenly aware that he outranked Lefferts and was inclined to be officious. As Emmons Clark puts it:

It must be confessed, that the officers of the Seventh Regiment and the patriotic citizens of Philadelphia, were not prepossessed in his favor, and his manners and appearance failed to remove the unfavorable impression. His personal appearance was far from attractive; in manner, he was captious and conceited, almost to rudeness; and his well-known political antecedents, as a Southern sympathizer, and as a supporter of slavery, the cause of the rebellion, were not calculated to secure the confidence of the unconditional and intensely loyal young men of the Seventh Regiment.[12]

Thus began a bitter feud between Butler and the Seventh Regiment, details of which have been picked apart endlessly in regimental histories, biographies of Butler, and his own memoirs. The General was a brilliant, highly talented lawyer, but unfortunately his whole career was marked by a series of quarrels and wranglings due to his aggressive manner and obstinacy. In this particular situation, however, the underlying difficulty may have been, not so much his personality, as the intense rivalry between the regiments, and between the states of Massachusetts and New York, to get full credit for bringing the first effective relief to Washington. In addition, it must be remembered that each regiment was operating under strict and urgent orders to get to Washington as quickly as possible, because the National Capital was in danger. In the absence of firm, overall direction from the Secretary of War, or General Scott, regimental commanders had to use their own best judgment in carrying out assignments. At this stage of the conflict troop movements were far from being part of a coordinated plan of the Army of the United States. Instead, they were a series of disjointed and independent state operations; each state and each military commander striving mightily to save the nation, with little or no cooperation among themselves, but nonetheless with intense patriotism.

Under these conditions it is not at all surprising that friction developed between Butler and Lefferts.

The first meeting of the two officers was brief. Butler asked Lefferts "what he proposed to do." The Colonel, who was at that time waiting for a reply to his telegrams, answered that he had not come to any decision but would wait for orders. This ended the interview, and Butler returned to his quarters. At eight-fifteen A.M. Lefferts, certain now that one way or another he would be in Annapolis, sent the following telegram to his brother-in-law:

> Philadelphia, Saturday morning,
> 8:15 o'clock, April 20, 1861
>
> W. H. Allen, 92 Beekman Street
> We cannot go by way of Baltimore. Will go to Annapolis. Require a good vessel and provisions to be sent there immediately. Go with this to William H. Aspinwall and General Sandford.
>
> M. Lefferts[13]

Probably the intention was still to go by rail to Perryville, but, as time passed with no reply from Washington, the idea of sailing direct from Philadelphia became more attractive. The prospect of finding the *Maryland* destroyed or disabled by the rebels could not be ignored. In fact, reports to that effect were already being circulated. After inquiring about other means of transport, Lefferts discovered that the steamer *Boston*, of the New York and Philadelphia line, was in port, ready to sail for New York. The officials of the company indicated that they would be willing to release her for charter. After further consultation with his officers who concurred heartily with the plan, Lefferts started arrangements for the charter of the vessel. Under the plan the Regiment would have the option of turning up the

Potomac, if it were open, or sailing up Chesapeake Bay to Annapolis.

General Butler reappeared at ten A.M. to try to persuade Colonel Lefferts to join with him in a concerted move to Perryville and from there to Annapolis. Lefferts heard him out but refused to change his plans. He pointed out the delay that would result from the impossibility of accommodating both regiments on the same trip in the *Maryland*, provided she were still available. Furthermore, the rumors were that the vessel had already been captured, and it might be necessary to move fifteen hundred men back to Philadelphia to start over again. Besides, Lefferts' orders were to report to the President as quickly as possible. He therefore refused absolutely to adopt an uncertain route that might delay him from carrying out his orders. Obviously angry at the refusal, Butler then departed with the Eighth Massachusetts by rail at eleven A.M.

In order to raise the necessary credit to charter the steamer, Lefferts then issued a draft on his own civilian firm in New York. The *Boston* was at the Jefferson Avenue wharf, filled with cargo for New York. Within the next four hours this cargo was removed from the holds, rations of beef and bread for three days purchased, and a supply of extra ammunition for muskets and howitzers procured. By three P.M. all was ready for departure. Meantime, Lefferts had sent another telegram to New York.

Philadelphia, 11 o'clock, April 20, 1861.

W. H. Allen.

We have chartered the steamer Boston, and shall try to go up to Washington. May return to Annapolis. Show this to same parties. For three hours, messages will reach me at steamer Boston, foot Spruce Street.

M. Lefferts.[14]

He also telegraphed the Secretary of War informing him of his intentions and requesting that a dispatch-boat meet him at the mouth of the Potomac, with orders as to the route to Washington.[15]

In the general confusion of these hours the reply from Washington to Lefferts' earlier telegram had reached Philadelphia but never quite caught up with him. The dispatch was sent to General Patterson:

> Adjutant-General's Office
> Washington, April 20, 1861
>
> Major-General Patterson, Philadelphia:
>   Send the troops now en route to this city by rail to Havre de Grace; thence by iron ferry-boat to Annapolis, as suggested by Colonel Lefferts. Report the time the troops may be expected at Annapolis. They should be prepared to march if cars cannot be provided.
>   Carry out vigorously the orders of the General-in-Chief to occupy the road to Baltimore.
>
> L. Thomas, Adjutant-General [16]

In his report to Thomas on April 21 Patterson reported his subsequent actions:

> On receipt of your telegram of yesterday I went to the transportation office and saw John Edgar Thomson and S. M. Felton, esqs., presidents of the Pennsylvania Central and the Philadelphia and Baltimore Railroads, and gave directions for the Eighth Massachusetts and Seventh New York to go via Annapolis to Washington. I could not find Colonel Lefferts, but saw General Butler, gave him the instructions, and desired him to communicate them to Colonel Lefferts.[17]

This telegram must have been received before eleven A.M., for Butler has reported that he left Philadelphia at that time. It is difficult to understand therefore why Patterson did not manage to deliver the orders to Lefferts in the next few hours. If they had been received, the Colonel was certainly running the risk of a court-martial by not going to Perryville. On the other hand it is quite conceivable that Patterson, when he talked to Felton and Thomson, realized that the Seventh Regiment was now so far committed to sailing from Philadelphia that it would be impossible to change plans. In that case, he may have decided not to expend too much effort in locating Lefferts. The main objective, after all, was to get men to Washington quickly, and there was not much sense in being fussy about a strict interpretation of orders.

Meantime, the Regiment was given no information about the reason for the delay, or their future movements. It would have been most imprudent to allow news of the route from Philadelphia to leak out to the public. Thus, the whole day was filled with wild rumors and endless speculation among the enlisted men. They slept in the railroad cars until dawn, when they were dismissed. The only immediate concern was breakfast and, after that, foraging for provisions to fill their knapsacks. Many of the men found themselves invited into private homes by hospitable Philadelphians, while others made their way to the Continental and Girard Hotels. At the Deaf and Dumb Asylum the Superintendent provided a beefsteak breakfast for any members of the Regiment who came by. Theodore Winthrop, with a couple of hundred others, headed up Broad Street to the Lapierre House.

> When I arrived I found every place at table filled and every waiter ten deep with orders. So, being an old campaigner, I followed up the stream of provender to the fountain-head, the kitchen. Half a dozen other old campaigners were already there, most hospitably entertained

by the cooks. They served us, hot and hot, with the best of the best, straight from the gridiron and the pan. I hope, if I live to breakfast again in the Lapierre House, that I may be allowed to help myself and choose for myself below-stairs.

When we rendezvoused at the tram, we found that the orders were for every man to provide himself three days' rations in the neighborhood, and be ready to start at a moment's notice.

A mountain of bread was already piled up in the station. I stuck my bayonet through a stout loaf, and with a dozen comrades armed in the same way went foraging about for other *vivers*.

It is a poor part of Philadelphia; but whatever they had in the shops or the houses seemed to be at our disposition.

I stopped at a corner shop to ask for pork, and was amicably assailed by an earnest dame,—Irish, I am pleased to say. She thrust her last loaf upon me, and sighed that it was not baked that morning for my "honor's service."

A little farther on, two kindly Quaker ladies compelled me to step in. "What could they do?" they asked eagerly. "They had no meat in the house; but could we eat eggs? They had in the house a dozen and a half, new laid." So the pot to the fire, and the eggs boiled, and bagged by myself and that tall Saxon, my friend E., of the Sixth Company. While the eggs simmered, the two ladies thee-ed us prayer-fully and tearfully, hoping that God would save our country from blood, unless blood must be shed to preserve Law and Liberty.[18]

During the morning at the depot the Seventh New York and the Eighth Massachusetts met for the first time and had the opportunity to size up each other. The mutual reaction was favorable. At the top, Lefferts and Butler might be feuding, but it was clear from the beginning that the "dandies" of the Seventh were going to get along famously with the sturdy fishermen from Gloucester and Marblehead, and the shoemakers from Lynn and Newburyport. The backgrounds of the two regiments were most dissimilar, but each saw something in the other that made for friendship. According to Fitz-James O'Brien's somewhat pompous comment,

> There was one peculiar difference that I noticed existing between the Massachusetts regiments that we met in Philadelphia and our men. The Massachusetts men—to whom all honor be given for the splendid manner in which they afterwards acted in a most trying situation—presented a singular moral contrast to the members of the Seventh. They were earnest, grim, determined. Badly equipped, haggard, unshorn, they yet had a manhood in their look that hardships could not kill. They were evidently thinking all the time of the contest into which they were about to enter. Their gray, eager eyes seemed to be looking for the heights of Virginia. With us, it was somewhat different. Our men were gay and careless, confident of being at any moment capable of performing, and more than performing, their duty. They looked battle in the face with a smile, and were ready to hob-knob with an enemy and kill him afterwards. The one was courage in the rough; the other was courage burnished. The steel was the same in both, but the last was a little more polished.[19]

At three P.M. the Regiment was ordered to "fall-in" and marched off down Washington Street to the wharf where the *Boston* was awaiting them. The ship was obviously too small to hold a thousand men comfortably and it took some time to squeeze everyone aboard. Eventually, however, the last man and the last piece of equipment was stowed away, and at 4:20 P.M. the ship left the dock and sailed down the Delaware. On shore "the multitude of spectators broke out into hearty cheers, and the men-of-war at the Navy Yard manned their yards and dipped their colors." [20] It was a lovely April afternoon and everyone was in high spirits despite the overcrowding which is vividly described by the regimental chaplain, Rev. Dr. S. H. Weston.

The boat was old and small, and even in smooth water careened so that the men had to be moved from side to side to keep her on an even keel. How so many could be crowded into such narrow quarters is still to me a mystery. What would have been the result, in the event of a heavy storm, it is fearful to contemplate. The lower hold, filled with men, was almost unendurable; with the hatches on, it would have been a "Black Hole." [21]

Fitz-James O'Brien goes on to describe the difficulties of sleeping on board:

We were obliged to sleep in all sorts of impossible attitudes. There is an ingenious device known to carpenters as "dove-tailing," and we were so thick that we had positively to dove-tail, only that there was very little of the dove about it; for when perambulating soldiers stepped on the faces and stomachs of the sleepers, as they lay on the deck, the greeting that they received had but little flavor of the olive branch.[22]

In the typical fashion of unseasoned regiments the commissary department had misjudged the food requirements in the haste to provision the ship. Rations were thus short, and, for supper, each man was issued a "piece of meat and a hard cracker." Even this, however, did not perturb them, as O'Brien points out.

Notwithstanding that we found very soon that the commissariat was in a bad way, the men were as jolly as sandboys. I never saw a more good-humored set of men in my life. Fellows who would at Delmonico's have sent back a *turban de volaille aux truffes* because the truffles were tough, here cheerfully took their places in file between decks, tin plates and tin cups in hand, in order to get an insufficient piece of beef and a vision of coffee. But it was all merrily done. The scant fare was seasoned with hilarity; and here I say to those people in New York who have sneered at the Seventh Regiment as being dandies, and guilty of the unpardonable crimes of cleanliness and kid gloves, that they would cease to scoff and remain to bless, had they beheld the square, honest, genial way in which these military Brummells roughed it.[23]

Fortunately the sea was unusually calm even after the vessel passed out of Delaware Bay into the ocean. At eleven A.M. on Sunday, April 21, Dr. Weston held Episcopal services on deck for the limited number that could get near enough to hear him. About noon, Cape Charles, at the tip of the peninsula, was sighted, and the ship changed course to enter Chesapeake Bay.

Colonel Lefferts at this point needed information badly. He would have to decide soon whether to turn up the Potomac to Washington, or continue on Chesapeake Bay to Annapolis. All the ships they had seen on the passage from Philadelphia had carefully avoided the *Boston*. Their Yankee skippers were probably taking no chances, even though she flew the Union flag, lest the ship be a secessionist transport. One trading schooner, however, came within hailing distance just before the *Boston* entered Chesapeake Bay. From the captain it was learned that "the Norfolk Navy-Yard had been burned, and the secessionists were capturing all the vessels in Hampton Roads." [24] What had happened was a blow to the Union. Commodore Charles S. McCauley, Commandant of the Navy Yard, under the threat of capture by Virginian forces, had been tricked into scuttling the fleet, including the *Merrimac*, instead of executing orders to send them to sea. Thus, Commodore Hiram Paulding, coming down from Washington in the *Pawnee* to relieve McCauley, had to set fire to as many ships as possible and to destroy the arsenal buildings, in order to prevent the Confederates from acquiring a ready-made navy. As it was, he was only partially successful. The rebels occupied the arsenal and acquired abundant artillery and other material, including the *Merrimac* which was later raised and put into service.

As already noted, Colonel Lefferts, before leaving Philadelphia, had telegraphed the Secretary of War asking for a dispatch boat to meet him, either off Fort Monroe or at the mouth of the Potomac, with orders as to the route he should follow to Washington. The telegram did not get through because of the destruction of the lines between Havre de Grace and Washington. Thus when the *Boston* passed the Chesapeake Bay light-ship there was no dispatch boat, or information from any source. The ship therefore headed up Chesapeake Bay towards the Potomac.

The best estimate of the situation could lead only to the conclusion that it was imprudent to attempt sailing up the river, unless definite information was obtained that it was open. If Virginian troops were strong enough to threaten the Norfolk Navy Yard, it was probable that they had set up fortifications at points along the Potomac. Fort Washington, for example, was known to be weakly defended, and it was conceivable that the rebels might have seized it already. The *Boston* was unarmed and hopelessly overloaded. Lefferts could lose his whole force, if he tried to run past a few shore batteries. Certainly, they would have no chance to fight back, penned up in the plodding old coastal steamer.

The only solution therefore was to keep on to Annapolis and proceed overland to Washington. This line of reasoning was confirmed by Colonel Samuel R. Curtis, who had been invited at Philadelphia to accompany the Regiment to Washington. Curtis was a West Point graduate who commanded the Second Ohio Regiment in the Mexican War with considerable success. He was now in his third term in Congress, as Republican representative from Iowa, but had resigned to become Colonel of the Second Iowa. Later he was promoted to Brigadier-General, and finally Major-General, after the successful Battle of Pea Ridge, March 6-8, 1863. With his advice, Lefferts felt reassured that his decision was correct.

At nine P.M. the mouth of the Potomac was passed with no sign of a dispatch boat. The *Boston* therefore remained on course, and about midnight was at the entrance to the Severn River. It was impossible to make the approach into Annapolis harbor in the dark, so the engines were slowed "and she crept forward at a snail's pace waiting for the day." [25]

V Annapolis

THE PRE-DAWN FOG in Annapolis Harbor was heavy on the morning of April 22. It lifted slightly, however, shortly after dawn, as the *Boston* crept in cautiously. The first thing visible was a large sailing-vessel at anchor. Immediately everyone suspected that it might be a secessionist ship, but, as the distance lessened, the Stars and Stripes became visible and the tension died down. Soon a hail came from the ship, "Let go your anchor!" No one on the *Boston*, however, could understand the signal and she continued on course. Soon repeated orders and much frantic hand signaling came from the naval vessel, which could now be identified as a frigate. Finally, her ports were opened and the guns run out. The *Boston* then slowed down, and an exchange of hails took place. "Are you the Seventh Regiment of New York?" "Yes!" "Let go your anchor and send an officer on board." Soon after, a boat was lowered, and a naval officer boarded the *Boston* with a request that Colonel Lefferts accompany him. The ship was "Old Ironsides," the U.S.S. *Constitution*, which was at that time being used as a school ship by the Naval Academy. Half a mile distant lay a long steamer, aground on a mud bank. Those familiar with the Philadelphia and Baltimore Railroad were immediately able to identify her as the ferry-boat *Maryland*. With the aid of a glass it was possible to see that the Eighth Massachusetts was on board. In the distance could be seen the buildings of the Naval Academy and the old city of Annapolis.[1]

The Eighth Massachusetts had reached Perryville at six P.M. on the twentieth to find the *Maryland* waiting for them, as planned by S. M. Felton. With difficulty the 724 men were packed on board and they set off for Annapolis. The boat was desperately overcrowded and the shortage of provisions was even worse than on the *Boston*. Colonel Lefferts might be accused of acting too impetuously at Philadelphia, but it was fortunate that he did. If the *Maryland* had been required to transport both regiments, it would have been necessary to make three round trips between Perryville and Annapolis.

By this time Annapolis and the surrounding country were seething with secessionism. The rails on the line from Annapolis to Annapolis Junction had been torn up. Many of the officers and students at the Naval Academy were Southern sympathizers and had departed for their home states. Most of the residents of the area were also strongly secession-minded and were threatening to seize the Academy and the frigate *Constitution*. Aware of this Gideon Welles, Secretary of the Navy, had requested the War Department to use some of the troops due at Annapolis in their defense. Thus, when Butler arrived, he was faced with an immediate request from Captain George S. Blake, superintendent of the Naval Academy, for help in towing the *Constitution* to safety in the harbor. Without bothering to land his troops, he ordered the *Maryland* to tow "Old

Ironsides" from its mooring and eventually managed to get her into deep water. Unfortunately the *Maryland* on the return trip ran aground on a mud shoal. All efforts to dislodge her proved fruitless, and the Eighth Massachusetts was therefore condemned to spend all day Sunday, and a good part of Monday, cooped up under frightful conditions. Butler had run into heavy opposition from the Governor of Maryland, the Mayor of Annapolis, as well as the Army Quartermaster at the post, all of whom vigorously protested his landing the Regiment. Thus he spent all Sunday wrangling with them, while the troops waited helplessly for some means of disembarking.

Aboard the *Constitution* Colonel Lefferts was advised not to attempt a landing until he had consulted the officials of the Naval Academy who could inform him about the state of affairs in the city. Accordingly he landed with several of his officers to examine the situation. First, however, he left orders for the *Boston* to make the attempt to free the *Maryland* from the mud bank. Theodore Winthrop has recounted the attempt:

> We could see them, half a mile off, making every effort to lighten her. The soldiers tramped forward and aft, danced on her decks, shot overboard a heavy baggage-truck. We saw them start the truck for the stern with a cheer. It crashed down. One end stuck in the mud. The other fell back and rested on the boat. They went at it with axes, and presently it was clear.
>
> As the tide rose, we gave our grounded friends a lift with a hawser. No go! The Boston tugged in vain. We got near enough to see the whites of the Massachusetts eyes, and their unlucky faces and uniforms all grimy with their lodgings in the coal-dust. They could not have been blacker, if they had been breathing battlesmoke and dust all day. That experience was clear gain to them." [2]

Ashore, Colonel Lefferts took the opportunity of sending off a dispatch to General Sandford informing him of the movements of the Regiment. He also attempted to clear up the somewhat cryptic note sent to his brother-in-law on the twentieth.

> I sent a cipher-despatch yesterday to W. H. Allen, 92 Beekman Street, the translation of which I requested might be handed to you, and also to William H. Aspinwall. I fear, however, that some trouble may have been experienced in making it out. I therefore repeat the substance of it.

Lefferts then proceeds to explain his actions in Philadelphia. He had drafted the note at three P.M. April 21. The dispatch continues:

> . . . I have decided to go on as far as the mouth of the Potomac, and, should there be no Government vessel there, shall proceed to Annapolis to keep open that line of communication,—an indispensable necessity in future operations. Upon arriving at Annapolis, I shall of course be guided by circumstances. We may have to march from thence to Washington, without Government controls the railroad. [sic] Of course I am placed in a very embarrassing position, but must do the bert I can, keeping in view the object we had when we started. I forgot to say that in the cipher despatch to W. H. Allen I requested that you would immediately cause a vessel with supplies to be sent to Annapolis, as it is only a town of some eight hundred inhabitants, and those not friendly; and, should we be compelled to intrench ourselves at that place, we might have difficulty in provisioning.
>
> Monday morning, 8:30 o'clock
>
> We have arrived at Annapolis, and find some of the Massachusetts troops here. We shall land, and endeavor

to make our way to Washington. We should have reinforcements and provisions sent here at once. I can give no
further information. There is considerable excitement.

M. Lefferts, Colonel.[3]

He also prepared a telegram to be sent through General
Butler, addressed to Secretary Cameron:

My command, about one thousand strong, arrived and
ready for duty. All well. Provisions short. Colonel Curtis,
who is with me, volunteers in any capacity.[4]

At the Naval Academy Colonel Lefferts and his officers
were met by the Mayor of Annapolis who made a formal
protest against the landing of the Regiment and predicted
"a bloody and difficult march through the State, should one
be attempted." Lefferts was disinclined to believe him, but
his assertions were confirmed by Captain Blake and the
other Academy officers, who insisted that any march would
be hotly contested. In reply to this Lefferts remarked that
his orders were to go through to Washington, and that he
intended to carry them out, using force if necessary.[5]

At some time during the morning Colonel Lefferts also
called on General Butler who was at the Academy. Butler
had sent a message earlier to the Colonel while he was still
on the *Boston:*

Will Colonel Lefferts, Honorable Mr. Curtis, and Captain Hamilton do me the favor to accompany me and my
detachment in our landing at Annapolis, and give me the
benefit of their advice and assistance.[6]

At the conference Lefferts agreed to allow the *Boston* to be
used for landing the Eighth Massachusetts as soon as the
Seventh could be disembarked.[7] They then returned to the
Boston, shortly after noon, to start landing operations. One

more attempt, however, was made to float the *Maryland*. The effort was completely unsuccessful and was abandoned after several hours. Finally at five P.M. the *Boston* reached its wharf and the Regiment was marched to the lawn that sloped down from the Academy buildings to the Severn River. The stores and camp equipment were then unloaded, and

A large detail was at once put on guard, at the dock, over the baggage and stores, and around the temporary encampment and its stacked arms; another detail was made for fatigue duty in unloading the steamer, so giving a broad hint to the new campaigners that a good soldier must occasionally be something of a porter; and there was soon, too, a busy attendance on the company messes, with "buckets of cooked meat and crackers." Then the men bade good by to their transport Boston, which Colonel Lefferts sent back to the aid of the Massachusetts men, all of whom were landed before dawn.[8]

Coffee was served to the Regiment by the cooks of the Naval Academy, and by nightfall the entire force was quartered in the fort and the recitation halls. A portion of the men were invited by the hospitable midshipmen to share their own rooms.

After forty-eight hours of discomfort the Regiment thus settled down to a peaceful night, happy to be freed at last from the overcrowded transport. At the command level, however, the sparks were beginning to fly as the Butler-Lefferts feud broke out once more. This time General Butler took the firm position that, as the ranking officer present, he had the right to issue orders to the Seventh Regiment. He based his attitude on the Articles of War of 1795 which provided that:

If, upon marches, guards, or in quarters, different corps of the army happen to join or do duty together, the officer highest in rank of the line of the army, marine corps or militia, by commission, there on duty or in quarters, shall command the whole, and give orders for what is needful to the service, unless otherwise specially directed by the President, according to the nature of the case.[9]

Colonel Lefferts, on the other hand, saw no reason to put himself under the General's command. Neither the Seventh New York nor the Eighth Massachusetts were as yet mustered into the actual service of the United States, and in Lefferts' opinion he was responsible to Governor Morgan, just as Butler was responsible to Governor Andrew of Massachusetts. He would, of course, take direct orders from Secretary Cameron or General Scott, but he saw no reason to accept them from a brigadier-general of state militia. His approach was the same as that of Major-General Patterson in Philadelphia when he hesitated to issue orders to the state troops concerning the route to Washington.

Early in the day on April 22 General Butler, therefore, issued Special Brigade Order, Number Thirty-Seven, which prescribed company drills at five A.M., set up regulations for stacking arms, lauded the Eighth Massachusetts for saving the *Constitution*, and warned against any "unauthorized interference with private property." The Seventh was included at the end:

> Colonel Lefferts command not having been originally included in this order, he will be furnished with a copy for his instruction.[10]

Next came another special order, which is undated but was probably issued in the early morning hours of Tuesday, April 23:

Headquarters Brigade United Militia, 1861
SPECIAL BRIGADE ORDER, No. 38

Colonel Lefferts's command will report themselves ready for such duty as shall be assigned them at half past eight o'clock this morning.[11]

By command of
B. F. Butler, Brigadier-General
W. H. Clemence, Brigade-Major.

By the next morning, the twenty-third, he had reached Order Number Forty-Five.

Headquarters Brigade U.S. Militia,
Annapolis, Md., April 23, 1861.
SPECIAL BRIGADE ORDER, No. 45

The General commanding the 3d Brigade orders that no officer or private belonging to his command suffer himself to leave the grounds belonging to the United States government, without a special requisition from him. Colonel Munroe of the Eighth and Lefferts of the Seventh Regiments will see that the execution of this order is strictly complied with in their respective commands.[12]

By order of
B. F. Butler
Brigadier-General of 3d Brigade
W. H. Clemence, Brigade-Major

This continuous flow of orders was received by the Seventh with mounting irritation, and Lefferts, apparently with the unanimous agreement of his officers, decided to ignore them. The major controversy, however, once more concerned the route to Washington. There were two choices. The troops could march overland along the wagon road between Annapolis and Washington, a distance of approximately thirty-five miles. According to the scanty information that could be obtained, however, the indications were that the march would be bitterly resisted; "that the whole country was in arms; that the roads were infested with guerrillas and bushwhackers." [13] Besides, there was a supply problem. Wagons and horses would have to be procured to transport supplies, baggage, and ammunition; additional rations must be purchased or seized; transportation for the sick, and possibly the wounded, must be provided. The alternative was to move by way of the Annapolis and Elk Cliff Railroad which ran from Annapolis to Annapolis Junction, and then transfer to the Washington Branch of the Baltimore and Ohio Railroad. The principal difficulty with this choice, however, was that reliable information had been received that the tracks were torn up between Annapolis and the Junction. This would mean a time-consuming repair job that would result in delaying the relief of Washington. On the other hand, repair of the railroad was essential in order to ensure the effective transportation of the regiments that were moving into Annapolis on the heels of the Seventh New York and the Eighth Massachusetts. Suddenly, with Baltimore blocked off, Annapolis had become a key transportation center for Northern troops.

Evidently with this in mind, and also because he had discovered that transport wagons were not available, General Butler had decided that the advance should be along the railroad. He planned on repairing the tracks as they moved along and seizing whatever rolling-stock was to be found. Both in his report to General Patterson on April 24 and in his memoirs he emphasizes his impatience to move the regiments and the immediate steps he took to seize the railroad. Unfortunately his accuracy is somewhat clouded by the statement in the Abstract of the Operations of the

Massachusetts Troops, published by the State of Massachusetts on the twenty-fourth in which it was announced that

> General Butler and his forces on Tuesday evening were awaiting the arrival of the Fifth (Massachusetts) Regiment, with its accompanying artillery, battery, and rifle battalion, upon the arrival of which, together with the New York regiments which departed for Annapolis on Sunday and Monday, they would be fully able to open and maintain communication between Annapolis and Washington.[14]

Whatever his intention, Butler, nevertheless, had made a correct estimate of the situation. As it turned out, the all-important consideration was to secure the line of communication between Annapolis and Washington, and both regiments were to act jointly in the operation.

On Monday evening, however, Colonel Lefferts and his officers were convinced that they should try the overland march to the Capital. Basically, their decision was based on their orders to get to Washington as quickly as possible. All the events of the last few days, the disorders in Maryland, the imminent secession of Virginia, could lead only to the conclusion that the Capital was in danger of attack. The Seventh, therefore, would move by the most direct route possible. Along with this motive was an increasing irritation with Butler and an intense desire to reach Washington before the Eighth Massachusetts. Accordingly, it was decided soon after landing to march the following morning, as soon as supplies and transportation could be procured. Whether or not Lefferts had in mind to wait for reinforcements, as Butler claims,[15] is difficult to determine. The Regiment was short of ammunition, and Lefferts would have to take into consideration the possibility that there would be fighting on the overland march.

The clash over these conflicting opinions was not long in coming. General Butler tried to convince Colonel Lefferts that the Seventh should march out along the railroad and start repairing the tracks. Lefferts wanted no part of this project but did acquiesce in Butler's request for permission to address the officers of the Seventh. According to Butler's version of the incident he spoke to them "on the necessity of an immediate march for the relief of Washington," and thought he had gotten their assent.[16] Clark, however, in his regimental history makes no mention of this but indicates that Butler was trying to patch up his differences with the Regiment:

> His appearance, manner, and general conduct, both at Philadelphia and in the bay of Annapolis, had rendered him extremely unpopular among all with whom he came in contact, both citizens and soldiers. Such being the apparent state of public opinion, it was not without some embarrassment that he commenced his speech to the officers of the Seventh Regiment. It is safe to say that, in all his oratorical efforts, he was never more successful. With flattering reference to the fair fame and patriotism of the Seventh Regiment, and to the courage and endurance of his "plain Massachusetts boys"; with well-worded expressions of patriotism and devotion to the country and love for the Union and its flag; with apt allusions to the historical past, to the momentous present, and to the future, so dependent upon the acts and efforts of the soldiers of New York and Massachusetts—he won the hearts of his hearers and disarmed them of their prejudices. It was no trifling victory, for he established in the minds of all who listened that character for energy and ability which he has since maintained before the American people, and which is so brilliant and commanding that it obscures his faults and imperfections.[17]

The success of this oratory was short-lived, however, for as soon as Butler left for his quarters Lefferts called the officers together for a consultation. He pointed out that this was an attempt by Butler to gain ascendancy over the Seventh, that he had been receiving a stream of orders from Butler during the day, that it was absurd for an officer in the militia of one state to claim authority over the militia of another, neither being yet in the United States service. After some discussion the officers unanimously supported this view and agreed, once more, that unless some assurance was received that Washington was safe, "Butler's proposition to march by railroad, laying the track, was not to be thought of; that, on the contrary, the turnpike must be taken, in order to reach Washington at the earliest practicable hour." [18]

Colonel Lefferts then went off to see General Butler, accompanied by Colonel Curtis. The session was stormy. As Butler describes it,

The trouble with Lefferts appeared to be that he had picked up somewhere a man who had once been at West Point, to accompany and cosset him in his command. Lefferts never called upon me without him, and he was at times somewhat officious, and not always too courteous. But I pardoned that on account of the color of his nose, and because I was not seeking difficulties.[19]

According to Butler's version, Lefferts informed him that his officers declined to march, whereupon the General lectured him on the method of giving orders and pointed out that as Brigadier-General he was issuing an order to march. This provoked a heated exchange with Colonel Curtis, or "Red Nose," as Butler calls him, on the Articles of War, until finally Butler ordered him out of the room. It is probable that it was at this conference that Butler ordered

Lefferts to detail two companies to seize the railroad depot at Annapolis and hold the property found there.[20] There is, however, some contradiction between the account in Butler's report to General Patterson and his memoirs.[21]

Clark's report of Colonel Lefferts' statement to General Butler is as follows:

> Colonel Lefferts, by the advice of his officers, stated to General Butler that the Seventh Regiment had been ordered by the Governor of New York to report direct to General Scott at Washington; that it had not placed itself or been placed by any order of the War Department under the command of any militia officer of the State of Massachusetts; that, while no order from General Butler could be received or obeyed, it was most anxious to co-operate with the troops of Massachusetts or any other loyal State in any and every effort designed for the speedy relief of Washington or the general welfare of the country; that, as the first to land at Annapolis, it was entitled to the advance in the forward movement; and that, being a large, well-equipped, thoroughly disciplined regiment, it was qualified to meet and overcome opposition, and would be of great service at the capital.[22]

Indignant and angry at this statement, Butler threatened to report the disobedience of his orders to the War Department. He then closed the conference and went back to the *Boston* to check on the landing of the Eighth Massachusetts.

While Lefferts would not accept orders from Butler, he did nevertheless send two or three men to check on the depot. They found everything quiet there, with a watchman on duty. It seemed unnecessary therefore to take any further action, and Lefferts let the matter rest. During the night, however, Butler sent two companies of the Eighth Massachusetts to seize the depot and march out two miles along the railroad. At the depot they found a small, rusty, dismantled locomotive. Butler, who was with the detachment, recalls the incident:

> I turned to the men, who stood in line in front of the depot, and said: "Do any of you know anything about such a machine as this?"
>
> Charles Homans, a private of Company E, stepped forward and took a good look at the engine and replied: "That engine was made in our shop; I guess I can fit her up and run her."
>
> "Go to work, and pick out some men to help you."
>
> Homans at once began his work, and in a short time the missing parts were found, adjusted, and the engine was in usual repair.[23]

Butler then assigned twenty experienced men to begin the task of laying track and sent a detachment out on reconnaissance under Lieutenant-Colonel Hincks. In the morning at six A.M. he received Lefferts' official reply to his order of the previous evening:

> Annapolis Academy, Monday night, April 22, 1861
>
> General B. F. Butler
>
> Commanding Massachusetts Volunteers:
>
> Sir: Upon consultation my officers do not deem it proper, under the circumstances, to co-operate in the proposed march by railroad, laying track as we go along, particularly in view of a large force hourly expected, and with so little ammunition as we possess. I must be governed by my officers in a matter of so much importance. I have directed this to be handed to you upon return from the transport ship.
>
> I am, sir, yours, respectfully,
> Marshall Lefferts
> Colonel, Seventh Regiment[24]

Theodore Winthrop remembers April 23 fondly:

> The day was halcyon, the grass was green and soft, the apple trees were just in blossom: it was a day to be remembered.
>
> Many of us will remember it, and show the marks of it for months, as the day we had our heads cropped.
>
> By evening there was hardly one poll in the Seventh tenable by anybody's grip. Most sat in the shade and were shorn by a barber. A few were honored with a clip by the artist hand of the *petit caporal* of our Engineer Company.[25]

It was also monotonous waiting for the orders to march, and, in order to relieve any impatience, a drill and parade were ordered, which terminated with a review by Captain Blake. "The leading citizens of the town were admitted with their families to the grounds, most of them secessionists, and were charmed with the excellent music of the band, and astonished at the drill and formidable appearance of so large a body of active, well-disciplined soldiers." [26] Meantime, the Quartermaster and his party were scouring the country for supplies and wagons with little or no success. Most of the residents were unsympathetic to the Union cause, and even those who were willing to sell demanded exorbitant prices. Besides, after his heavy expenses in Philadelphia, Lefferts was running short of funds.

Early in the day, a messenger arrived from Washington. It was Frederick W. Lander, who had been sent by General Scott to discover the reasons for the delay of the regiments. Lander was a railroad surveyor for the government who had made several transcontinental expeditions for the proposed Puget Sound–Mississippi River railroad and was often entrusted with important missions for the Army. Scott, needing men badly in Washington, had already sent eight mes-

sengers to Annapolis, but only Lander and one other were
able to get through. Lander reported that

> he had been taken prisoner by a large party of secession-
> ists, and that all the roads were infested with troopers and
> armed men, and that in his opinion, derived from personal
> observation, the Regiment would meet with serious re-
> sistance upon the road to Washington, and could not
> expect to reach that point without a loss of a large number
> of men. Yet so perilous was the situation of affairs at
> Washington that he advised a forward movement at any
> cost; and, as it was impossible to make suitable provision
> for the conveyance of sick or wounded men, that they be
> left upon the road, to the mercy and humanity of the
> Marylanders.[27]

This news must have upset Lefferts considerably. He
had insufficient ammunition; his men were unseasoned
and far from ready for action, despite their confident high
spirits. Nevertheless, he apparently was now all the more
convinced that his regiment would have to march over the
wagon road to Washington.

Some time later, however, another messenger arrived in
Annapolis. He reported that Washington was still safe, but
it was important to reach there at the earliest possible moment. His dispatches recommended that the troops should
use the railroad route via Annapolis Junction, repairing the
tracks as they moved along, so that transportation for the
regiments following the Seventh and the Eighth would be
available. Thus, the plan of the Seventh had to be abandoned and the route decided upon by General Butler
accepted. This change, of course, relieved all tension between the regiments, and, from this moment on, their
cooperation with each other was notable. The identity of

the second messenger is not disclosed by the early historians of the Regiment, but it is quite possible that it was Captain Morris S. Miller, Assistant Quartermaster of the United States Army, who was ordered to Annapolis on the twenty-second.[28]

By sunset plans were completed, and it was announced that two companies would advance along the railroad, to be followed by the remainder of the Regiment and the Eighth Massachusetts at daylight. The Second Company, under Captain Emmons Clark, and the Sixth Company, Captain Benjamin M. Nevers, Jr., were detailed as the advance units. Colonel Lefferts then sent off the following dispatch to Governor Morgan:

Annapolis, April 23d, 1861

His Excellency
   E. D. Morgan
Sir:—Upon the arrival of my command at Philadelphia, I found it impracticable to reach Washington via Baltimore, and, after waiting eight hours for answer from the Sec. of War, I made up my mind, from all the information I could gather, that Annapolis would of necessity become a most important point or military base. And I immediately chartered a steamer and embarked for this place—and was the first to land, and feel I have already done some little service to the Government. The Mass. troops, or, at least, a portion of them, passed from Phil. via Havre de Grace— and tomorrow morning at daylight I leave for Washington via Annapolis & Baltimore R.R.—and may have to march 40 miles, as the people have torn up rails, bridges, etc. And we shall also have fighting. I have yesterday and to-day had couriers from Washington, and I am directed to press on. I have been detained twenty four hours for want of sufficient funds to provision the men for 3 days march. I hear to-day of fresh troops to arrive, and in my judgment

they are needed here to replace us, as soon as we leave, so as to keep the communication open. I have had to purchase supplies, charter steamer, etc. And I desire your Excellency will place to my credit, in such way as my drafts will be honored, an amount of Ten Thousand dollars (10,000). Of course the proper vouchers will in all cases accompany the drafts. We shall in all probability have further expenses. And exigency of the case admits of no delay, and this is the reason for my requests. You will please address me at Washington. And I remain,

Your Excellencies
Ob. Servant
Marshall Lefferts
Col. 7 Regt. N.Y.S.M.[29]

The Regiment was now ordered to get as much rest as possible in anticipation of the march on the following day. About eleven P.M., however, a general alarm was sounded: the "long roll" of the regimental drums. Immediately, everyone sprung up from their resting places, and within a short time the Regiment was formed into companies. Even the midshipmen were alerted, and dashed down the hill with their howitzers. It was rumored that an attack from the city was expected, but no one could detect any signs of movement in the slumbering town. Finally it was discovered that several ships had entered the harbor. Rockets had been sent up from the *Constitution*, as arranged by the officers of the Naval Academy. It was the *Baltic* and several other vessels, carrying the Sixth, Twelfth, and Seventy-first New York State Militia. Butler and Lefferts would no longer have to worry about reinforcements, and the march could begin.

VI The March to Annapolis Junction

WASHINGTON WAS now closer to panic than it had ever been. The news of the rioting in Baltimore on the nineteenth had been startling indeed, but the impact was not truly felt in the city until Sunday, April 21. It was then that people began to realize they were cut off from the North. Mail was not coming in; no trains were running; supplies of food began to dwindle. Monday brought more bad news. Following the lead of Colonel Robert E. Lee, who had resigned his commission in the United States Army on the twentieth, scores of government officials and high-ranking Army and Navy officers submitted their resignations and departed for the South. It was also a day of wild rumor, of frightening reports that an attack on the city was close at hand. On Tuesday a delivery of New York mail, three days old, was received, including newspapers telling of Anderson's enthusiastic reception in New York, the departure of the Seventh, the mass meeting in Union Square, and the general wild uprising of the people in the Northern States. All of this was most inspiring, but where were the troops? If they were at Annapolis, could they not even march twenty miles to the Junction?

President Lincoln, ordinarily calm and self-possessed, had

worked himself into a state of extreme nervous tension. On the twenty-second Scott informed him of the probability that Fort Washington was being attacked, that rebel troops were erecting a battery four miles below Mount Vernon, that cars had been sent up to Harpers Ferry to transport two thousand other troops in a general attack on the Capital. He assured him, however, that he could defend the Capitol, the Arsenal, and all the executive buildings against ten thousand troops "not better than our District Volunteers." But, when Mr. Lincoln thought he heard the booming of cannon and went out to the Arsenal to investigate, he found the doors wide open and no guards on duty. He needed men, and needed them quickly. The five companies of Pennsylvania troops and the Sixth Massachusetts Militia were just a drop in the bucket. Still, he was grateful to them, and when some wounded soldiers of the Sixth visited him on the twenty-fourth, he paid them a notable compliment: "I begin to believe that there is no North. The Seventh regiment is a myth. Rhode Island is another. You are the only real thing."

The Seventh was real enough, and so was the Eighth Massachusetts. At that moment they were pushing doggedly along the railroad from Annapolis. The advance guard of the Seventh was ready to move at four A.M. on Wednesday, April 24. The battalion consisted of the Second and Sixth Companies, together with a detachment from the Tenth, under Lieutenant T. B. Bunting. It had been decided that one of the howitzers should go out with the advance. As senior officer, Captain Nevers, Sixth Company, was in command. "Leaving the beautiful grounds of the Naval Academy, the detachment moved through the narrow and crooked streets of the city, past ancient, elegant, and substantial dwellings, past the old State-House where

Washington delivered his farewell address and resigned his commission as commander-in-chief of the American army, and up the hill to the little depot of the Annapolis and Washington Railroad." [1] There they found the Massachusetts detail that had been working all the previous day on the old locomotive. With infinite patience and ingenuity they had reassembled, cleaned, and oiled the parts, and it was now working handsomely. They had even managed to restore the first two miles of railroad track. Private Homans, by now the hero of the day, was happily perched in the cab, as engineer, and no one dared dispute his claim.

A novel train was now assembled. First came two open platform cars, which they improvised by sawing off the tops of two cattle cars. On the first was mounted the howitzer, loaded with grape, guarded by sixteen men from the Tenth, eight on each side. At the forward end Bunting acted as conductor, waving signals to the engineer. The second car carried the ammunition for the howitzer and a guard of six riflemen. Next came the locomotive, followed by two small passenger cars into which were jammed the Second and Sixth Companies. By now it was broad daylight and the train moved slowly towards the Junction, the locomotive wheezing slightly but otherwise performing nobly. Two miles out they found the picket-guard of the Eighth Massachusetts, under Lieutenant-Colonel Hincks. They had been without food for nearly a day and, by now, were thoroughly miserable. Seeing their condition the New Yorkers immediately opened up their knapsacks and generously shared rations with them. Their gratitude was overwhelming. If any barrier of hostility between the two regiments had seeped down into the ranks, this gesture now dispelled it completely. In fact, throughout the entire march, the Seventh went out of its way to share provisions with the inadequately supplied Eighth. Fitz-James O'Brien, who marched out with the main body, writes:

> These brave boys, I say, were starving while they were doing this good work. What their Colonel was doing, I can't say. As we marched along the track that they had laid, they greeted us with ranks of smiling but hungry faces. One boy told me, with a laugh on his young lips, that he had not eaten anything for thirty hours. There was not, thank God, a haversack in our regiment that was not emptied into the hands of these ill-treated heroes, nor a flask that was not at their disposal. I am glad to pay them tribute here, and mentally doff my cap.[2]

The result was an unshakeable friendship between the two regiments that lasted throughout the entire stay at Washington.

The Massachusetts detachment now moved ahead with Nevers' battalion. Progress was now slowed down, however, because it became necessary to replace rails at various places. About three miles out they found a small body of men busily at work ripping up more track. Immediately, Lt. Noah L. Farnham of the Second and Lt. Richard F. Halsted of the Sixth were sent out with a detail to capture them. Before they could be reached, however, the men managed to escape into the woods. Nevers now decided that he had best move forward without the locomotive and passenger cars, which could be better defended if they remained where they were. The two platform cars were therefore uncoupled and drag-ropes attached to them. The battalion then moved on, pulling along the two cars. Again it was necessary to stop from time to time to repair the track.

The battalion had been ordered to advance about six miles, then halt, and await the arrival of the remainder of the Regiment. This point was reached about nine A.M. and a halt was ordered. A detail was sent ahead to reconnoitre but found only mounted citizens fleeing from the advancing troops. Nearby was a log house which Lieutenant Bunting set off to explore:

> Having nothing to eat, I took twelve men and went to a house on the top of the hill, where we could see all around the country for some distance. Saw nothing of the enemy, so we knocked at the door. No answer. Opened the door, and went in. Found the house empty. Looked in the cupboard and found some preserves. We ate them in short order. Looked under the bed, and found a basket of eggs (hens', ducks', and turkeys'), which we sucked. Then we found a second cupboard, and in it some fat bacon. This we sent after the eggs and preserves, and were ready for either a fight or a march. As we were getting ready to leave, a man came rushing in, in great haste and much scared. We extended the hospitalities of the house to him, and he took a seat. We soon ascertained that he was the proprietor, and that his family had got scared and run into the swamp. Sent him after them, when they returned. We recounted the damage we had done, and told the old fellow to fix his price. He said we were heartily welcome,— we knew he lied,—and that the things were worth probably $3. We gave him $10, and he was the happiest man in the State.[3]

Oddly enough, on the wall hung a picture of Colonel Abram Duryee, ex-Commanding Officer of the Regiment. Colonel Hincks and Captain Clark, who came in at this point, were able to persuade the owner to unearth more supplies by the "pleasant jingly of silver, and the flavor of wine from Clark's flask." He also told them that the whole region was alarmed by the warlike demonstrations from

Annapolis and that there was a large armed force at the Junction.

Back at Annapolis the main body of the Regiment was aroused at dawn and ordered to prepare for the march. "Blankets and overcoats were rolled up and strapped upon knapsacks; canteens were filled with water tinged with vinegar; three days' rations, consisting of six navy biscuit and pieces of raw salt pork or beef, were served to each man; cartridges were distributed, and guns loaded, for the start." [4] Colonel Lefferts, relieved now that he was finally able to move his regiment, sent a message to the *Baltic* in an attempt to obtain additional supplies. Colonel Daniel Butterfield of the Twelfth New York State Militia was happy to oblige and asked him to requisition what he needed. He also landed nine more men of the Seventh Regiment whom he had brought on from New York. There were four newly arrived vessels in the harbor now; three of them containing the New York regiments, and the fourth with the First Rhode Island Militia, led by Governor Sprague in person. Convinced now that his rear was protected and that communications would remain open, Lefferts marched out with his regiment at eight A.M. The officers' baggage and camp equipment were left behind, including a "thousand velvet carpet-covered camp stools," as General Butler recalls gleefully in his memoirs. [5]

Captain Clark's account of the next few hours follows:

> The march of six miles in the extreme heat was not without its effect upon the young and inexperienced soldiers, already debilitated, by confinement on the steamer Boston, change of diet, and want of rest; yet they struggled manfully forward, and but few were obliged to fall out and wait for the train which was to follow. About ten o'clock the main body reached the bivouac of the advance-guard, and,

as it approached upon the railroad-track, marching by the flank, with its bright bayonets glistening in the sunlight, its appearance was peculiarly imposing and formidable. The Second and Sixth Companies now formed and again took the advance, accompanied by a platform-car with its howitzer. With the main body, which followed at no great distance, was another platform-car for the sick or wounded and for medical stores; and a third, containing the remaining howitzer and its ammunition, brought up the rear. Upon a railroad-track where the ties were laid upon the surface, through deep cuts and over an arid soil, under a noonday sun, and with the thermometer above 90°, the Regiment pushed gallantly forward. As the engine and passenger-cars had been sent back for the use of the Eighth Massachusetts, now also on its march from Annapolis, the platform-cars afforded the only accommodations for those prostrated by fatigue and heat. Halting frequently to search for missing rails and to repair the track, the Regiment averaged only about one mile per hour, and it was after 2 P.M. that it reached a water-station known among the natives of that vicinity as Millersville.[6]

Theodore Winthrop had not gone out with the first howitzer. With the remainder of the Ninth Company, he marched out in the morning:

After a few minutes' halt, we hear the whistle of the engine. This machine is also an historic character in the war.

Remember it! "J. H. Nicholson" is its name. Charles Homans drives, and on either side stands a sentry with fixed bayonet. New spectacles for America! But it is grand to know that the bayonets are to protect, not to assail, Liberty and Law.

The train leads off. We follow, by the track. Presently

the train returns. We pass it and trudge on in light marching order, carrying arms, blankets, haversacks, and canteens.
Our knapsacks are upon the train.

Fortunate for our backs that they do not have to bear
any more burden! For the day grows sultry. It is one of
those breezeless baking days which brew thundergusts.
We march on for some four miles, when, coming upon
the guards of the Massachusetts Eighth, our howitzer is
ordered to fall out and wait for the train. With a comrade
of the Artillery, I am placed on guard over it.

Henry Bonnell is my fellow-sentry. He, like myself, is an
old campaigner in such campaigns as our generation has
known. So we talk California, Oregon, Indian life, the
Plains, keeping our eyes peeled meanwhile, and ranging
the country. Men that will tear up track are quite capable
of picking off a sentry. A giant chestnut gives us little dots
of shade from its pigmy leaves. The country about us is
open and newly ploughed. Some of the worm-fences are
new, and ten rails high; but the farming is careless, and
the soil thin.

Two of the Massachusetts men come back to the gun
while we are standing there. One is my friend Stephen
Morris, of Marblehead, Sutton Light Infantry. I had
shared my breakfast yesterday with Stephen. So we re-
fraternize.

His business is,—"I make shoes in winter and fishin'
in summer." He gives me a few facts,—suspicious persons
seen about the track, men on horseback in the distance.
One of the Massachusetts guard last night challenged his
captain. Captain replied, "Officer of the night." Whereupon says Stephe, "The recruit let squizzle and jest missed
his ear." He then related to me the incident of the railroad station. "The first thing they know'd," says he, "we
bit right into the depot and took charge." "I don't mind,"
Stephe remarked,—"I don't mind life, nor yit death; but

whenever I see a Massachusetts boy, I stick by him, and if them Secessionists attackt us to-night, or any other time, they'll git in debt."

Whistle, again! and the train appears. We are ordered to ship our howitzer on a platform car. The engine pushes us on. The train brings our light baggage and the rear guard.

A hundred yards farther on is a delicious fresh spring below the bank. While the train halts, Stephe Morris rushes down to fill my canteen. "This an't like Marblehead," says Stephe, panting up; "but a man that can shin up them rocks can git right over this sand."

The train goes slowly on, as a rickety train should. At intervals we see the fresh spots of track just laid by our Yankee friends. Near the sixth mile, we began to overtake hot and uncomfortable squads of our fellows. The unseasonable heat of this most breathless day was too much for many of the younger men, unaccustomed to rough work, and weakened by want of sleep and irregular food in our hurried movements thus far.

Charles Homans's private carriage was, however, ready to pick up tired men, hot men, thirsty men, men with corns, or men with blisters. They tumbled into the train in considerable numbers.[7]

Millersville was just a water-station on the railroad line with little to distinguish it except a bridge, crossing the stream just beyond the station. At a little after two P.M. the column reached the station and came to an abrupt halt. The bridge had been completely destroyed and would have to be rebuilt before the Regiment could move on. It was obvious that this would take several hours, since the bridge was twenty feet high and sixteen feet long. Besides, the Seventh had never yet been called upon to construct a bridge, and it was with some misgivings that the

Tenth Company, as the Engineer Corps, prepared for the job. Before they could start, however, they had to wait out a storm which suddenly descended on the Regiment, thoroughly drenching everyone. Although a pleasant relief to the heat at the time, it added considerably to their discomfort during the cold of the following night. Winthrop tells the story of the bridge-building:

When the frenzy of the brief tempest was over, it began to be a question, "What to do about the broken bridge?" The gap was narrow; but even Charles Homans could not promise to leap the "J. H. Nicholson" over it. Who was to be our Julius Caesar in bridge-building? Who but Sergeant Scott, Armorer of the Regiment, with my fellow-sentry of the morning, Bonnell, as First Assistant?

Scott called for a working party. There were plenty of handy fellows among our Engineers and in the Line. Tools were plenty in the Engineers' chest. We pushed the platform car upon which howitzer No. 1 was mounted down to the gap, and began operations.

"I wish," says the *petit caporal* of the Engineer Company, patting his howitzer gently on the back, "that I could get this Putty Blower pointed at the enemy, while you fellows are bridge-building."

The inefficient destructives of Maryland had only half spoilt the bridge. Some of the old timbers could be used, —and for new ones, there was the forest.

Scott and his party made a good and a quick job of it. Our friends of the Massachusetts Eighth had now come up. They lent a ready hand, as usual. The sun set brilliantly. By twilight there was a practicable bridge. The engine was despatched back to keep the road open. The two platform cars, freighted with our howitzers, were rigged with the gun-ropes for dragging along the rail. We passed through the files of the Massachusetts men, resting by the way, and eating by the fires of the evening, the suppers we had in great part provided them; and so begins our night-march.[8]

Any lingering resemblance to the annual encampments of the Regiment now disappeared completely as the Seventh pushed on in the fading twilight. Annapolis was only twelve miles away, but the railroad had to be put back into operation and progress was unbearably slow. For those detailed to the task of laying track the march meant searching all over the countryside for the missing rails, then fitting and fastening them into place. "Sometimes the search was a long one, sometimes it was but a few rods distant in the hollow of a neighboring field. . . . In one place about twenty feet of track, rails, chairs, and ties, had been lifted up, and pitched to the bottom of the steep embankment. The howitzer ropes were fastened upon this section, and it was hauled up into place." [9] Others had the irksome task of dragging and pushing forward the platform-cars on which the howitzers and caissons were mounted. For the main body of the Regiment, however, the march consisted of a series of short movements forward followed by frequent halts, during which most of the men fell asleep instantly. As Fitz-James O'Brien describes it;

> As the night wore on, the monotony of the march became oppressive. Owing to our having to explore every inch of the way, we did not make more than a mile or a mile and a half an hour. We ran out of stimulants, and almost out of water. Most of us had not slept for four nights, and as the night advanced our march was almost a stagger. This was not so much fatigue as want of excitement. Our fellows were spoiling for a fight; and when a dropping shot was heard in the distance, it was wonderful to see how the languid legs straightened, and the column braced itself for action. If we had had even the small-

est kind of skirmish, the men would have been able to
walk to Washington. As it was, we went sleepily on. I
myself fell asleep walking in the ranks. Numbers, I find,
followed my example.[10]

Theodore Winthrop has also left a brilliant account of
the night march:

O Gottschalk! what a poetic Marche de Nuit we then
began to play, with our heels and toes, on the railroad
track!

It was full-moonlight and the night inexpressibly sweet
and serene. The air was cool and vivified by the gust and
shower of the afternoon. Fresh spring was in every breath.
Our fellows had forgotten that this morning they were hot
and disgusted. Every one hugged his rifle as if it were the
arm of the Girl of his Heart, and stepped out gayly for the
promenade. Tired or footsore men, or even lazy ones,
could mount upon the two freight-cars we were using for
artillery-wagons. There were stout arms enough to tow the
whole.

The scouts went ahead under First Lieutenant Farnham
of the Second Company. We were at school together—
I am afraid to say how many years ago. He is just the same
cool, dry, shrewd fellow he was as a boy, and a most efficient
officer.

It was an original kind of march. I suppose a battery of
howitzers never before found itself mounted upon cars,
ready to open fire at once and bang away into the offing
with shrapnel or into the bushes with canister. Our line
extended a half-mile along the track. It was beautiful to
stand on the bank above a cutting and watch the files strike
from the shadow of a wood into a broad flame of moon-
light, every rifle sparkling up alert as it came forward. A
beautiful sight to see the barrels writing themselves upon
the dimness, each a silver flash.

By-and-by, "Halt!" came, repeated along from the front, company after company. "Halt! a rail gone."

It was found without difficulty. The imbeciles who took it up probably supposed we would not wish to wet our feet by searching for it in the dewy grass of the next field. With incredible doltishness they had also left the chairs and spikes beside the track. Bonnell took hold, and in a few minutes had the rail in place and firm enough to pass the engine. Remember, we were not only hurrying on to succor Washington, but opening the only convenient and practicable route between it and the loyal States.

A little farther on, we came to a village,—a rare sight in this scantily peopled region. Here Sergeant Keeler, of our company, the tallest man in the regiment, and one of the handiest, suggested that we should tear up the rails at a turn-out by the station, and so be prepared for chances. So "Out crowbars!" was the word. We tore up and bagged half a dozen rails, with chairs and spikes complete. Here, too, some of the engineers found a keg of spikes. This was also bagged and loaded on our cars. We fought the chaps with their own weapons, since they would not meet us with ours.

These things made delay, and by-and-by there was a long halt, while the Colonel communicated, by orders sounded along the line, with the engine. Homans's drag was hard after us, bringing our knapsacks and traps.

After I had admired for some time the beauty of our moonlit line, and listened to the orders as they grew or died along the distance, I began to want excitement. Bonnell suggested that he and I should scout up the road and see if any rails were wanting. We travelled along into the quiet night.

A mile ahead of the line we suddenly caught the gleam of a rifle-barrel. "Who goes there?" one of our own scouts challenged smartly.

We had arrived at the nick of time. Three rails were up.

Two of them were easily found. The third was discovered by beating the brush thoroughly. Bonnell and I ran back for tools, and returned at full trot with crowbar and sledge on our shoulders. There were plenty of willing hands to help,—too many, indeed,—and with the aid of a huge Massachusetts man we soon had the rail in place.

From this time on we were constantly interrupted. Not a half mile passed without a rail up. Bonnell was always at the front laying track, and I am proud to say that he accepted me as aide-de-camp. Other fellows, unknown to me in the dark, gave hearty help. The Seventh showed that it could do something else than drill.

At one spot, on a high embankment over standing water, the rail was gone, sunk probably. Here we tried our rails brought from the turn-out. They were too short. We supplemented with a length of plank from our stores. We rolled our cars carefully over. They passed safe. But Homans shook his head. He could not venture a locomotive on that frail stuff. So we lost the society of the "J. H. Nicholson." Next day the Massachusetts commander called for some one to dive in the pool for the lost rail. Plump into the water went a little wiry chap and grappled the rail. "When I come up," says the brave fellow afterwards to me, "our officer out with a twenty-dollar gold piece and wanted me to take it. 'That a'n't what I come for,' says I. 'Take it,' says he, 'and share with the others.' 'That a'n't what they come for,' says I. But I took a big cold," the diver continued, "and I'm condemned hoarse yit,"—which was the fact.

Farther on we found a whole length of track torn up, on both sides, sleepers and all, and the same thing repeated with alternations of breaks of single rails. Our howitzer-ropes came into play to hoist and haul. We were not going to be stopped.

But it was becoming a Noche Triste to some of our comrades. We had now marched some sixteen miles. The

distance was trifling. But the men had been on their legs
pretty much all day and night. Hardly any one had had any
full or substantial sleep or meal since we started from New
York. They napped off, standing, leaning on their guns,
dropping in their tracks on the wet ground, at every halt.
They were sleepy, but plucky. As we passed through deep
cuttings, places, as it were, built for defence, there was a
general desire that the tedium of the night should be
relieved by a shindy.

During the whole night I saw our officers moving about
the line, doing their duty vigorously, despite exhaustion,
hunger, and sleeplessness.

About midnight our friends of the Eighth had joined
us, and our whole little army struggled on together. I find
that I have been rather understating the troubles of the
march. It seems impossible that such difficulty could be
encountered within twenty miles of the capital of our
nation. But we were making a rush to put ourselves in that
capital, and we could not proceed in the slow, systematic
way of an advancing army. We must take the risk and stand
the suffering, whatever it was. So the Seventh Regiment
went through its bloodless Noche Triste.[11]

During one of the halts, about midnight, some of the
members of the Second Company were attempting to
open a large box containing railroad tools, and one of their
muskets was accidently fired. This caused no alarm in the
immediate vicinity, but the skirmishing party out ahead,
commanded by Lieutenant Farnham, at once supposed that
the Regiment was about to be attacked. They, therefore,
fired several muskets and pistols as a

signal that they were not far distant, from which, however, the Regiment naturally inferred that the skirmishers
had met the enemy and were in danger of being over-
powered. Captains Nevers and Clark, with a part of their

commands, immediately hastened forward to reconnoitre and to support Lieutenant Farnham and his men, and met them hastening back to the Regiment. Not expecting to meet friends coming to their assistance, it was only by the merest chance that a collision was avoided. The two parties had approached in the darkness to within twenty yards of each other, muskets were cocked and at a ready, and Lieutenant Farnham was about to give the command to fire when a familiar voice was recognized, and a serious loss of life was providentially prevented.[12]

At length, between three and four o'clock the Regiment emerged from the woods and swamp into a wheat field about a mile from the Junction. Lieutenant Farnham and his skirmishers had, a short time before, dashed into the little village and found it unoccupied, except for the sleeping residents. Colonel Lefferts then took a detachment of 150 men ahead to investigate further, but the expected opposition failed to materialize. Returning to the Regiment he then allowed fires to be built of the neighboring fence-rails. As usual, the Seventh, before they left, sought out the owners and paid liberally for the damage. As for provisions, the people of Annapolis Junction proved unexpectedly friendly, and, within a short time, were parading out, offering bread, milk, eggs, chickens, etc., for sale.

On April 24 General Scott had sent out a train from Washington to meet the Seventh, and information was obtained that it would probably come again sometime before noon. For a few hours, therefore, the Regiment had an opportunity to rest after the toils of the previous night. The Second Company had meantime moved into the Junction and were stretched out on the railroad platforms in an exhausted sleep. Some of the men, however, were detailed to advance on a small hand-car towards Washington to meet the expected train, or to hasten it forward in case it had not yet left the city. After six miles of laborious pumping they met the train, in charge of the National Rifles, Captain Smead commanding, and returned with it to the Junction. By ten o'clock the whole Regiment had been crowded into the cars. The train then left for Washington, arriving there at noon on April 25.

VII Arrival in Washington

WASHINGTON AWAKENED gloomily again on the morning of Thursday, April 25. The flip of a coin was still as good a method as any for determining who would get there first. Was it to be a relieving column from the North, pounding along Bladensburg Road or clambering down from the cars at the Baltimore and Ohio depot; or would Long Bridge hear the thud of an invading rebel detachment from across the Potomac? From the President on down the whole city was aware of the clamor in the South for an immediate attack. Copies of the Richmond *Examiner* for April 23 were available, with its editor screaming that "the capture of Washington City is perfectly within the power of Virginia and Maryland," and that "our people can take it— they will take it—and Scott the arch-traitor, and Lincoln the Beast, combined, cannot prevent it."

General Scott had disposed his pitifully small forces, as best he could, at strategic points throughout the city, with a Regular Army officer in command at each place. General Lorenzo Thomas commanded in Georgetown; Major Irvin McDowell, at the Capitol; the paymaster, Major David Hunter, was assigned to the President's mansion, with Colonel Charles P. Stone defending Executive Square. At the Post Office, the State Department, the Treasury Building, the Patent Office, the Smithsonian Institution, and at several other points, were the remaining staff officers.[1] At the Long Bridge, Company E, Second Artillery, Capt. J. Howard Carlisle commanding, stood guard. The Sixth Massachusetts was at the Capitol, with the Pennsylvania troops, but was alerted to move to the President's mansion in case of attack. Senator-elect James H. Lane, the Kansas border fighter, had put together a battalion called the Frontier Guards, and Cassius M. Clay had delayed his departure to the post of Minister in Russia in order to form Clay's Battalion. These two groups were assigned to the Navy Yard.[2] All in all Scott had managed well, but it was evident even to the militarily untutored public that this motley array of government clerks, laborers, foreign residents, and doddering veterans of the War of 1812, even with the regular companies and the state militia, would be helpless in the face of enemy attack. And General Scott was busy preparing his General Orders Number Four for the following day: "From the known assemblage near this city of numerous hostile bodies of troops it is evident that an attack upon it may be expected at any moment."[3]

Relief came at noon. Looking northeast along the tracks, the crowd at the railroad depot could see no sign of a train, but they could hear the chugging engine and its welcome whistle as it turned down Delaware Avenue. Finally, they could see the long line of cars making the turn at Massachusetts Avenue. They were overflowing with soldiers, and, as the train approached, it was possible to make out the gray uniforms and white cross-belts of the New York Seventh. Outside the Capitol, a block away, some men of the Sixth Massachusetts spotted them at the same time and a mighty shout went up that echoed through

Recruiting Office in City Hall Park, New York.

Tompkins Market Armory, New York City, 1861. This armory was erected for the Seventh Regiment, which occupied it from 1860 until 1880. It was subsequently used by the Sixty-ninth Regiment.

After the great mass meeting in Union Square, New York, April 20, 1861.

Knots of citizens still linger around the stands where Anderson, who had abandoned Sumter only six days before, had just roused the multitude to wild enthusiasm. Of this gathering in support of the Government the *New York Herald* said at the time: "Such a mighty uprising of the people has never before been witnessed in New York, nor throughout the whole length and breadth of the Union. Five stands were erected, from which some of the most able speakers of the city and state addressed the multitude on the necessity of rallying around the flag of the Republic in this hour of its danger. A series of resolutions was proposed and unanimously adopted, pledging the meeting to use every means to preserve the Union intact and inviolate. Great unanimity prevailed throughout the whole proceedings; party politics were ignored, and the entire meeting—speakers and listeners—were a unit in maintaining the national honor unsullied. Major Anderson, the hero of Fort Sumter, was present, and showed himself at the various stands, at each of which he was most enthusiastically received. An impressive feature of the occasion was the flag of Sumter, hoisted on the stump of the staff that had been shot away, placed in the hand of the equestrian statue of Washington."

General veiw of Annapolis, with the *Constitution* in the fore-ground.

The practice battery at Annapolis.

Target practice from the Naval battery.

The Seventh Regiment on board the *Boston* en route for Annapolis.

The Seventh Regiment New York State Militia halting for a rest on the march to Annapolis Junction.

Courtesy of Harper's Weekly

The railroad depot, Washington, D.C., April 1861.

Courtesy of Harper's Weekly

Camp Cameron, Georgetown, D.C., the encampment of the
Seventh Regiment.

Courtesy of Harper's Weekly

Service by Reverend Dr. Weston, Chaplain of the Seventh
Regiment, at Camp Cameron on Sunday, May 5, 1861.

United States Volunteers throwing up intrenchments on
Arlington Heights.

The advance guard of the Grand Army of the United States
crossing the Long Bridge over the Potomac, at two A.M. on May
24, 1861.

Courtesy of The New-York Historical Society, New York City

Colonel Marshall Lefferts.

Brigadier General Benjamin F. Butler, commanding Massachusetts Militia.

Private Lyman Tiffany, Seventh Company. Washington, D.C.,
April 1861.

De Witt C. Falls, Sixth Company. Washington, D.C., April 1861.

1. R. W. Bootman, 2. R. N. Bowerman, 3. Wm. Turner, 4. E. T. Putnam, 5. T. E. Hathaway, 6. S. J. Sherman, members of the Seventh Company. Washington, D.C., April 1861.

A sergeant and five privates of the First Company take their
ease at Camp Cameron, May 1861.

U.S. Signal Corps photo

Members of the Seventh Regiment at Camp Cameron.

Guard Tent, Seventh Regiment, Camp Cameron.

Company Street, Camp Cameron.

Photo by John F. Carroll

April 19, 1961—New York City's Times Square is temporarily renamed Seventh Regiment Square in honor of the departure of the first New York citizen soldiers to respond to President Lincoln's call.

Photo by John F. Carroll

April 19, 1961—Veterans of the Seventh Regiment placing wreaths on Civil War Statue of Seventh Regiment Soldier in New York's Central Park.

the city. Within a few minutes the streets were filled as
the news spread, and Washington began to realize that its
five days of isolation were ended.

The men of the Seventh may have been tired from their
unaccustomed hardships of the night before, but never
could they resist the opportunity to parade. Besides, Colonel Lefferts had been ordered to report to the President
of the United States, and anything less than a march down
Pennsylvania Avenue to the White House would have ill-
become the Seventh's sense of fitness. So, after an hour of
brushing uniforms and wiping off cross-belts and trotting
out the little brass howitzers, off they went, proud of
themselves and their regiment. As the New York *Tribune*
reported on the following day:

> At one o'clock the regiment was on the Avenue, march-
> ing in splendid style toward the White House. They looked
> worn and weary, as well they might, after their rough
> work. Nevertheless, they were all in good spirits, and they
> walked almost with springing steps. As they passed along,
> they were received with frequent cheers, and the ladies con-
> tinually waved their handkerchiefs, while smiles were on
> every face. No body of men could ever meet a more enthu-
> siastic or hearty greeting than they, to whom every bosom
> seemed to warm. When in place of the drums and fifes, the
> full band struck up, the whole city danced with delight.
> A greater change never passed over a town, than that
> wrought in the space of half an hour by the coming of the
> long-looked-for Seventh.[4]

At the White House they passed in review before the
President, and Secretaries Seward and Cameron. "Mr. Lincoln," according to the New York *Tribune*, "was the happiest-looking man in town as the regiment was marching by
him. As an Illinois man remarked, 'He smiled all over,' and

he certainly gave in his countenance clear expression to the
feeling of relief born in all by this wished-for arrival." [5] Mrs.
Lincoln was there also and presented the Regiment with a
magnificent bouquet from the conservatory of the White
House.

Looking back on the event some years later, Mr. Lincoln's secretaries sum it up as follows:

> Those who were in the Federal capital on that Thurs-
> day, April 25, will never, during their lives, forget the event.
> An indescribable gloom had hung over Washington nearly
> a week, paralyzing its traffic and crushing out its life.
> As soon as the arrival was known, an immense crowd
> gathered at the depot to obtain ocular evidence that relief
> had at length reached the city. Promptly debarking and
> forming, the Seventh marched up Pennsylvania Avenue
> to the White House. As they passed up the magnificent
> street, with their well-formed ranks, their exact military
> step, their soldierly bearing, their gayly floating flags, and
> the inspiring music of their splendid regimental band, they
> seemed to sweep all thought of danger and all taint of
> treason out of that great national thoroughfare and out of
> every human heart in the Federal city. The presence of this
> single regiment seemed to turn the scales of fate. Cheer
> upon cheer greeted them, windows were thrown up, houses
> opened, the population came forth upon the streets as for
> a holiday. It was an epoch in American history. For the
> first time, the combined spirit and power of Liberty
> entered the nation's capital. [6]

The Regiment was now dismissed, and the companies
marched off to quarters assigned to them at Willard's, at
the National, and at Brown's Hotel. The primary concern
of everyone was to wash off the grime that had been acquired in the mud of Maryland and all the hotel baths soon

had long lines in front of them. At Willard's the huge fountain in the court was the center of attraction and soon became an impromptu shower bath. The hotels then served them the first substantial meal they had eaten since the previous Friday, and the remainder of the afternoon was spent in letter-writing, seeking out barbers, sightseeing, and for most of the Regiment, finding some corner to catch a few hours of sleep.

Colonel Lefferts had remained at the White House with the President. Mr. Lincoln was much concerned about Maryland and questioned Lefferts intensively about the attitude of the citizens concerning secession. He also wanted to hear the full story of the march from Annapolis. After two hours the President closed the interview by complimenting the Regiment and thanking the officers and members "from the bottom of my heart." Colonel Lefferts then reported to General Scott for duty. The General was most cordial and said emphatically, "You have made a fine march, sir; you have done all that could be done, and you have my thanks." [7] Scott was particularly pleased when Lefferts reported that his camp equipment would soon be arriving from Annapolis and that the Seventh would require nothing from the government except rations.

The War Department had decided some time earlier to use the Capitol building, and a few other public buildings, as quarters for the incoming troops. The hasty mobilization and the urgency of the need for men to defend Washington meant that the States would be sending on badly equipped militia units and newly formed volunteer organizations. Perhaps one or two of the regiments might be ready to go into camp within a few days; for the vast majority it would be a matter of weeks before the proper equipment could be obtained. Some of the regiments would even come in with a good portion of their men lacking uniforms. Even the Seventh New York, probably the best-equipped of all, would have to be quartered until their camp equipage could be moved from Annapolis where it had been left behind.

In 1861 the Capitol was far from complete, despite the work of the previous ten years. The two new wings had been added and decorated ornately. A short time before, the Senate Chamber and the Hall of Representatives had been occupied by the legislators. In the center the old dome had been removed, but only the base of the new one had been installed. The grounds were cluttered with supply sheds and piles of materials, blocks of marble, lumber, and metal plates. There was some concern about the possible damage that might occur with troops occupying the lavishly decorated interior, but in the emergency the government had no other choice. It was hoped that the building would be cleared by July 4 when Congress returned. The Sixth Massachusetts was therefore assigned to the Senate Chamber and the Seventh New York to the Hall of Representatives. The Eighth Massachusetts, when it arrived, was to be quartered in the center under the open dome.

Towards evening the Companies were again assembled and marched off to their new quarters. Theodore Winthrop tells the story:

> We marched up the hill, and when the dust opened there was our Big Tent ready pitched.
> It was an enormous tent,—the Sibley pattern modified. A simple soul in our ranks looked up and said,—"Tent! canvas! I don't see it: that's marble!" Whereupon a simpler soul informed us,—"Boys, that's the Capitol."
> And so it was the Capitol,—as glad to see the New York Seventh Regiment as they to see it. The Capitol was

to be our quarters, and I was pleased to notice the top of the dome had been left off for ventilation. . . .

They gave us the Representatives Chamber for quarters. Without running the gauntlet of caucus primary and election, every one of us attained that sacred shrine.

In we marched, tramp, tramp. Bayonets took the place of buncombe. The frowzy creatures in ill-made dress-coats, shimmering satin waistcoats, and hats of the tile model, who lounge, spit, and vociferate there, and name themselves M.C., were off. Our neat uniforms and bright barrels showed to great advantage, compared with the usual costumes of the usual *dramatis personae* of the scene.

It was dramatic business, our entrance there. The new Chamber is gorgeous, but ineffective. Its ceiling is flat, and panelled with transparencies. Each panel is the coat-of-arms of a State, painted on glass. I could not see that the impartial sunbeams, tempered by this skylight, had burned away the insignia of the malcontent States. Nor had any rampant Secessionist thought to punch any of the lost Pleiads out from that firmament with a long pole. Crimson and gold are the prevailing hues of the decorations. There is no unity and breadth of coloring. The desks of the members radiate in double files from a white marble tribune at the centre of the semicircle. . . .

Some of our companies were marched up-stairs into the galleries. The sofas were to be their beds. With their white cross-belts and bright breastplates, they made a very picturesque body of spectators for whatever happened in the Hall, and never failed to applaud in the right or the wrong place at will.

Most of us were bestowed in the amphitheatre. Each desk received its man. He was to scribble on it by day, and sleep under it by night. When the desks were all taken, the companies overflowed into the corners and into the lobbies. The staff took committee-rooms. The Colonel reigned in the Speaker's parlor.[8]

On the afternoon of Friday, April 26, 1861, the Seventh Regiment was mustered into the service of the United States. The regulations for mustering into service had been issued in 1848 and covered in precise detail the entire procedure of making muster-rolls, interview of candidates, inspection and enumeration of companies, and administration of the oath. In Washington, Major (soon to be Major-General) Irvin McDowell had been assigned as mustering officer. At three o'clock he appeared in Capitol Square where the companies had begun to assemble. With him were President Lincoln, Secretary of State Seward, Secretary of War Cameron, and several other officials. Apparently McDowell was impressed by what he saw. The Seventh was the Nation's crack parade regiment and rarely failed to arouse favorable comment. As McDowell passed the Second Company he turned to Captain Clark and exclaimed, "Sir, you have a company of officers instead of soldiers!" [9] The Regiment was then formed into line and broken into column by companies, following which Major McDowell called the rolls. The total strength of the Regiment at the time of muster was 1034 men.

Although the troops called for under the President's proclamation were supposed to be mustered in for three months, the Seventh was granted special consideration because they had departed for Washington immediately upon the reception of the proclamation. The general intention in New York was to recruit for each regiment men who were willing and able to volunteer for the full three month period. In the case of the Seventh, however, because of the special urgency of relieving Washington, almost the entire regiment had dropped everything, with little or no opportunity to arrange personal affairs, and hastened off to the

capital. It was expected that they would remain for a few
weeks until their place could be taken by other volunteer
units. When the Regiment was formed into a square,
Major McDowell, therefore, announced that "In accordance with a special arrangement made in your case with
the Governor of New York, you are now mustered into the
service of the United States to serve for thirty days, unless
sooner discharged. The magistrate will administer the
oath." [10] Private Winthrop was much impressed, as usual,
and has left an account of the ceremony:

> Hereupon a gentleman *en mufti*, but wearing a military
> cap with an oil-skin cover, was revealed. Until now he had
> seemed an impassive supernumerary. But he was biding
> his time, and—with due respect be it said—saving his
> wind, and now in a Stentorian voice he ejaculated,—
> *"The following is the oath!"*
> *Per se* this remark was not comic. But there was some-
> thing in the dignitary's manner which tickled the regiment.
> As one man the thousand smiled, and immediately
> adopted this new epigram among its private countersigns.
> But the good-natured smile passed away as we listened
> to the impressive oath, following its title.
> We raised our right hands, and, clause by clause, re-
> peated the solemn obligation, in the name of God, to be
> faithful soldiers of our country. It was not quite so compre-
> hensive as the beautiful knightly pledge administered by
> King Arthur to his comrades, and transmitted to our time
> by Major-General Tennyson of the Parnassus Division.
> We did not swear, as they did of yore, to be true lovers
> as well as loyal soldiers. *Ça va sans dire* in 1861,—particu-
> larly when you were engaged to your Amanda the evening
> before you started, as was the case with many a stalwart
> brave and many a mighty man of a corporal or sergeant in
> our ranks.

We were thrilled and solemnized by the stately ceremony of the oath. This again was most dramatic. A grand public recognition of a duty. A reavowal of the fundamental belief that our system was worthy of the support, and our Government of the confidence, of all loyal men. And there was danger in the middle distance of our view into the future,—danger of attack, or dangerous duty of advance, just enough to keep any trifler from feeling that his pledge was mere holiday business.

So, under the cloudless blue sky, we echoed in unison the sentences of the oath. A little low murmur of rattling arms, shaken with a hearty utterance, made itself heard in the pauses. Then the band crashed in magnificently.[11]

On the same day the Eighth Massachusetts arrived in Washington and was immediately quartered in the Capitol under the dome. The joint march from Annapolis had cemented the friendship between the two regiments, and on Saturday the twenty-seventh the officers and members of the Seventh invited the Eighth Massachusetts to a "grand collation." A letter from a member of the Seventh recalls the scene:

Just now, as I passed through the Rotunda, there was a non-commissioned officer mounted on the staircase to the dome, explaining to the Massachusetts men, who were drawn up in order around the Rotunda, what our men had done. In the centre were piled fifteen kegs of lager-beer, two thousand boiled eggs, piles of cheese, boxes of lemons and oranges, smoked beef, pipes and tobacco, bread, &c., and a squad of men of the Seventh had begun to draw and pass around the provender. It was hard to say which party looked the more delighted, the donors or the recipients.[12]

The recipients were evidently overjoyed, because, two days later, they adopted the following effusive resolution:

Headquarters, Commanders of Companies,
Eighth Regiment, M.V.M.,
Washington, April 29, 1861.

To Colonel Lefferts, Officers and Members of the New York Seventh Regiment:

At a meeting of this Regiment, held this morning, the following preamble and resolutions were unanimously adopted: Whereas, The trials and fortunes of war have brought us into close intimacy and companionship with the New York Seventh Regiment (National Guard), therefore

Resolved, That we feel it a duty owing not only to them, but to our own hearts, to express, so far as may be in our power, our grateful obligations to them for their many favors.

Resolved, That we deeply appreciate the hearty welcome extended to us on landing at Annapolis, and their kind attention after the fatigues of transportation and hazardous though successful service.

Resolved, That they have done all in their power to lessen the just feelings of dissatisfaction which have prevailed throughout the Regiment, by sharing with us their rations and their little conveniences, and by ever being the first to offer assistance.

Resolved, That especially are our thanks due to the noble Seventh for the generous entertainment furnished on the afternoon of Saturday, April 27th—an entertainment so spontaneous, so bounteous, so heartily appreciative of our condition, that no words can do it justice, or do justice to our gratitude.

Resolved, That in one other and very especial particular does their generosity and benevolence touch our hearts. We refer to the voluntary subscriptions raised among them for the benefit of one of our officers accidentally wounded.

Resolved, That the term of aspersion so often used in

connection with the volunteer militia, "holiday soldiery," has been, in all the conduct of the Regiment to which we are so much indebted, triumphantly refuted, and that it will hereafter be worthy of the highest fame—fame that will ever attach to the name of the "Generous, Gallant, Glorious Seventh."

Resolved, That wherever the Seventh may go we would go, where they lodge we would lodge, and, if ever their colors go down before the hosts of the enemy, the Eighth of Massachusetts would be the first to avenge their fall with the heart's blood of every man

Knott V. Martin, Chairman.

George T. Newhall, Secretary.[13]

Probably Ben Butler would not appreciate the reference to the "just feelings of dissatisfaction," but the Seventh received the communication with delight. The wounded officer was Lieutenant Herrick, for whom the Seventh raised by subscription the sum of five hundred dollars.

Saturday, the twenty-seventh, also saw the arrival in Washington of the *S.S. Daylight*, loaded with preserved meats, bread, vegetables, and other necessary stores for the Regiment. Aboard her were Capt. Egbert L. Viele, the regimental engineer, with an additional 175 men who had not been able to leave with the Regiment, and some recruits. The *Daylight* had left New York on April 24 and was the first unarmed vessel to reach Washington. Colonel Lefferts' telegrams of April 20 to his brother-in-law and his message to General Sandford on the twenty-first had been confusing, and there was some doubt as to whether the vessel should be sent to Annapolis or Washington. Aaron Kemp, the paymaster of the Regiment, had remained behind in New York, and set to work energetically as soon as news was received that supplies were needed. After a conference with the Quartermaster he visited the Chamber of Commerce, where a committee happened to be in session on Saturday, April 20. The Chamber again came to the rescue and presented Kemp with a check for $2500.00. During the next few days he solicited donations of supplies and funds from friends of the Regiment. By 2:30 P.M. on April 24 he was able to send the *Daylight* on its way, even managing to face down General Sandford who insisted on a delay until another vessel could accompany her. Meantime, Captain Viele was busy accepting some recruits and notifying the remaining members of the Regiment of their imminent departure. On the morning of the twenty-fourth, he assembled his detachment in the Armory and marched them off to the pier. Since they had missed the original muster, this detachment was mustered into federal service on April 30, 1861.[14]

Lefferts, of course, was much concerned about the mounting cost of keeping the Regiment in service. He had issued drafts on his own firm, in order to charter the *Boston* and, since the twenty-third, had been waiting eagerly for a reply from Governor Morgan concerning his request for ten thousand dollars. Morgan unfortunately was unable to accede the request and referred Lefferts to the War Department. The following is his letter received by Lefferts on the first of May:

> I hasten to reply to your letter of the 23d instant, written at Annapolis, Md., this moment at hand, requesting me to write to you at Washington.
> Approving as I do of the course adopted by you in making your way to Washington with the gallant regiment under your command, I have, in relation to the question of funds expended on your journey to Washington, to ask you to represent the case to the Secretary of War, who, I do

not doubt, will give directions for the immediate reim-
bursement of the sum thus expended.

You will without delay advise me of the result of such
application to the Secretary of War.

I am, &c., &c.,

E. D. Morgan[15]

This was most disappointing, but Colonel Lefferts immediately hurried off to the War Department and on the
same day reported to Morgan:

> I made application at the proper department to have the
> charter party of a vessel just arrived with stores for us
> assumed by them, which I urged upon the ground that
> she also brought troops. They informed me no doubt, at a
> future day, we would be refunded the outlay, but they
> would not pay now. This vessel and stores were sent by my
> directions when I expected to be hemmed in, perhaps for
> weeks. This vessel and cargo cost us $4,000 charter-party,
> and $8,000 for stores; there was so much confusion conse-
> quent upon the hurried manner in which troops have been
> sent forward, that it was absolutely necessary to make out-
> lays upon my own responsibility, or lie idly waiting for
> others to move. In order to save the government from all
> trouble for us, and when others actually required more
> attention, I said I would commute for my rations, and take
> care of ourselves. This costs us fifty cents per man, over and
> above the amount received for rations; it seems hard that
> I must call upon my men for money in such a case.
>
> I now leave the matter to be disposed of as you may
> deem best.[16]

Morgan may not have been able to help, but New York
City could, especially when their own Seventh was in
trouble. In a few days Lefferts once more heard from the
indefatigable Kemp:

My dear Colonel.,—Ere this reaches you, I presume you will have received my telegram saying the Union Defence Committee had given me a check for the full amount of the charter and the entire invoice of goods sent you. I think old Kemp deserves well of his regiment. He has worked night and day to bring the result of his expedition to a successful issue, and to-day his exertions are crowned with success; he has his money, and the Daylight is home, safe and sound. I won't annoy you with the detail of how I have been bamboozled about from one committee and sub-committee to another. These committees have been perfectly overwhelmed with work themselves, often till one and two in the morning; but I started to succeed and have. God bless my dear boys! If they only knew how, for days and days without news, the true, full heart of New York has beat for them, they and yourself would be proud of that magic figure *seven*. It pained me greatly to see in the papers that the Richmond Grays, Captain Elliot, were at Norfolk. When he was here, and we all swore devotedness to the Union, I presumed the flag borne in his command represented the flag of the Union. I little dreamed he would feel it his duty to fight under any other. . . .

A. Kemp, Paymaster, Seventh Regiment.[17]

On Sunday, April 28, the Regiment held Episcopal service in the Hall of Representatives, with Chaplain Sullivan H. Weston officiating in the morning and Dr. Sunderland of Washington in the evening. The Speaker's desk, covered with a flag upon which rested the Bible, was used as a pulpit. Within the Clerk's circle was a choir of twenty selected from the Regiment, while the band was stationed in the press gallery. The remainder of the Regiment, except two hundred on guard, occupied the floor and galleries.

The Regiment now settled down to a fairly routine existence for the next few days. Unlike most of the other regiments now pouring into the Capital the Seventh found a way to avoid the miserable ration of bacon and biscuit, prepared in the vaults beneath the Capitol. Much to the envy of less fortunate units, they marched down from Capitol Hill three times a day to the large hotels for meals. Captain Clark in his history of the Second Company describes a typical day:

At sunrise, the reveille is sounded, and drums from every part of the city, where troops are stationed, echo back the unwelcome morning music. From the Company quarters in the gallery, from the adjacent corridor, and from divers comfortable and uncomfortable nooks and corners, the members tumble up, half-asleep and half dressed, to answer roll-call. The orders for the day are promulgated by the orderly, and the men are dismissed and hasten away to secure an early chance at the baths and basins which munificent Congressmen had, in days of peace, provided for the people's representatives. While the younger members are enduring the tortures of squad drill, they who have passed that fiery ordeal read, write, lounge, smoke, and impatiently wait for breakfast. The long-looked-for hour at length arrives, the Company is formed, and marches down the hill in cadenced step, and with the steadiness and precision of veterans, to the Washington Hotel. The untutored soldiers from the several States, now daily an almost hourly increasing in number, halt and gaze with almost envious admiration at these handsome, well-drilled and well-dressed soldiers; the ladies, that have from choice or necessity remained in town, express in divers ways their favor and approbation; and staid and quiet citizens, with smiling faces and kind words, avow their confidence in their brave defenders. Appetites are sharpening under the influence of early rising, exercise, and regular habits, and the substantial fare at the Washington suffers severely whenever the Second Company darkens the door. Breakfast over, the Company marches back with the same precision to the Capitol. All turn out to witness guard mounting, and to listen to the splendid music of the band, and having secured available positions, quietly smoke their pipes, and criticise the movements of the old guard and the new. At 9 o'clock, a Company drill completes the military duties of the morning. Passes to visit the town are now in great demand. They who do not seek or obtain them, sleep upon the sofas, or dream in the shade of the fine trees of Capitol Square, or occupy Congressional chairs and write long epistles to friends at home. Letter writing is a decided mania, and members of Congress drop in, from time to time, and spend hours in franking the letters of the soldiers. The hour for dinner finds every one awake and ready, and the Company marches down the hill, in due time to march up again. The afternoon would drag heavily were it not for the inexhaustible fund of wit and humor, and the general capacity for amusement, for which the Seventh Regiment is distinguished. Private Hazens, of the Second Company, occupies the Speaker's chair, which he had seized at the earliest moment and held against all opposition, and from time to time the house is called to order; speeches from the members upon a variety of subjects are listened to with becoming gravity; the latest conundrums are propounded; songs, comic, patriotic and sentimental are sung, and with critical regard to merit, are applauded. No bores are tolerated by the young sovereigns, and he who fails to entertain is unceremoniously silenced by interruptions from the floor, or by paper missiles from the galleries. At length the mail arrives, and there is a grand rush to the Speaker's desk, from which are announced the names of those favored with letters from home. The fountains of love and affection, which sleep so quietly beneath the gray jacket of the soldiers, are now unlocked by fond words from mother, sister, wife or sweetheart, and the marble halls of the Capitol are consecrated by the sacred emotions of the heart, and by vows of eternal constancy. But the call for evening parade has sounded; letters are hastily folded and carefully laid aside; the neat white belts, with their bright brass plates are adjusted; muskets which defy the most rigid inspection are shouldered, and all hasten to the parade ground. The evening parade of a large fine regiment is always an interesting and imposing ceremony, and being a novelty in Washington at this time, attracts a large number of citizens, soldiers and government officials to Capitol Square. And the Seventh is proud of its evening parades, of its polished arms, its neat uniforms and its perfection in every detail, while the spectators look, wonder, and admire. The parade is over, and then to supper. In the evening, the hall is brilliantly lighted, and the amusements of the afternoon are repeated, until tattoo warns all that the labors and pleasures of the day are ended. Coats and boots come off with wonderful rapidity, and by the score and the hundreds; blankets appear and are carefully spread beneath the desks, in the aisles, upon the seats in the galleries, and upon the marble floors of the corridors; and at *taps,* the lights go out, and all except the guard are prepared for sleep. They who would continue to crack jokes, or in any way disturb the quiet of the hour, are silenced by the not very polite remonstrances of their comrades, or by the peremptory order of the sentinels, and at 11 P.M., the last and the least sleepy soldier is in the land of dreams. Should one drop in at midnight upon this hall with its thousand sleeping soldiers, he would be amused if not entertained at the variety of sounds that would greet his ear, from the quiet and gentle breathing of the easy sleeper far up the scale to the sonorous and trumpet-like tones of those noisy devotees of Morpheus who make night hideous. But dreams of home and of the future alone disturb this crowd of sleepers, until the unwelcome notes of reveille again summon them to the duties of another day.[18]

This monotonous routine was to last only until May 2. More and more troops were pouring into Washington and the Seventh, which now had its camp equipment, was not at all reluctant to give up its space in the Capitol. Before the *Daylight* sailed back to New York, it had picked up the equipment from Annapolis and the Regiment was now ready for camp.

VIII   Camp Cameron

THE SEVENTH had very positive military ideas on the subject of a secure and sanitary campsite. As the first regiment ready to move into camp, it had the first choice of sites and immediately sought out the best possible location. Colonel Lefferts and his officers, after investigating all possibilities, had chosen Dr. Stone's farm, on Meridian Hill, two miles north of Willard's on the Harpers Ferry road. The location was ideal. The farm contained about forty acres and commanded a splendid view of the city of Washington, of the Potomac, "stretching away like a beautiful lake to Alexandria," and of Arlington Heights in Virginia. On the estate was an elegant, old mansion, built by President Madison in the early years of the century and used by several Presidents as a summer residence. On the south side of the property was a large field eminently suitable as a parade-ground for the Regiment.

Although the owners had offered the site to the Regiment, Colonel Lefferts had some difficulty in obtaining War Department approval. Colonel Joseph K. F. Mansfield had been assigned to command of the Department of Washington on April 28, and Lefferts, accordingly, had to approach him for orders. On the thirtieth he informed

Colonel Mansfield that the camp equipage had arrived from Annapolis, adding, "I visited in person the grounds of Mr. Stone, suggested by Lieutenant-General Scott, as the place designated for an encampment, and am prepared to proceed and occupy the ground upon receipt of an order from you to that effect." Scott, however, must have changed his mind, for Mansfield returned the note to Lefferts with the following indorsement, "The General-in-Chief prefers that this regiment be camped at Fletcher's Kalorama, in rear of his house, represented to be a fine camping-ground. It is out on West 20th Street. Go and examine the premises, and, if suitable, go into camp there." [1] This was decidedly not suitable to Lefferts and he had to use all his influence to have the orders changed. Evidently, he managed to see the right persons, for Mansfield backed down and gave the Regiment authority to encamp on Meridian Hill.

Major McDowell was, at that time, in command of the Capitol Building. On May 1, therefore, Colonel Lefferts informed him of the move.

> In compliance with orders from head-quarters, I shall move my main body of troops to-morrow afternoon at half past three o'clock for encampment on Meridian Hill. I have detailed two of my companies for guard duty to-morrow, but have to ask whether you will give other directions or make arrangements to relieve my companies from duty during the day, that they may go with the main body to camp.
>
> Allow me at this opportunity to thank you most heartily for your many kind attentions, and express my regret at moving away from the building which has brought us into such close and pleasant contact. [2]

McDowell answered on the same day, as follows:

Head-quarters of the Capitol
May 1, 1861.

Colonel Marshall Lefferts, Seventh Regiment, N.Y.S.M.

Colonel.—Agreeably to the request contained in your note of this date, I have given directions that the companies of your regiment be relieved from the detail for guard to-morrow.

It is with sincere regret I find the hour for your departure at hand. It is a positive pleasure to have your regiment here, for I do not exaggerate when I say a finer body of a thousand men are not on the face of this globe.

With the kindest wishes for you all, I have the honor to be, Colonel,

Very respectfully, your most obedient servant,

Irvin McDowell.,
Assistant Adjutant-General[3]

Regimental orders were issued at evening parade on May 1, covering the movement of the following day:

By directions from head-quarters, the regiment will go into camp to-morrow at the farm of Mr. Stone, Meridian Hill. The hour of march will be stated in orders to-morrow morning.

Quartermaster Winchester is directed to have the camp equipage transported immediately to the place herein designated.

Lieutenant E. M. Le Moyne, commanding, will have his command ready for marching orders, with one day's rations, at three o'clock this P.M.

Captain Viele will accompany the command, and superintend the laying out of the camp.

Commissary Patten will cause the necessary stores to be transported from the Navy-Yard.[4]

At four P.M., therefore, on Thursday, May 2, the Seventh Regiment, minus the Ninth and Tenth Companies which had gone out to Meridian Hill the day before, said good-by to their Massachusetts friends and marched out of the Capitol. Their route took them down Pennsylvania Avenue and then up Fourteenth Street. In front of the National Hotel Governor Sprague's Rhode Island Regiment presented arms as they passed. Unfortunately the spell of warm and pleasant weather was about over, and, by nightfall when they reached Meridian Hill, the temperature had dropped almost to the freezing mark. The tents had been prepared for them, but the carpenters had not yet installed the floor-boards. Thus they settled down to a miserable night, which became even more so on the following morning when a cold north-east rainstorm began. To add to their miseries, the company kitchens had not been set up as yet, and rations had to be cooked on the small ranges in the Stone mansion. This meant that the companies had to line up in the mud and wait more or less patiently until food could be brought out to them. By Saturday, May 4, however, the storm had blown itself out and the Regiment settled down to make the camp livable. The floors were installed in the tents, the camp-stoves, two for each company, arrived, and within a week Camp Cameron was a model of luxurious outdoor living.

Camp Cameron, as it was called, in honor of the Secretary of War, was typical of most Civil War Camps, except that the Seventh, being a wealthy and exacting Regiment, and also a superbly trained one, had soon brought it to a peak of military efficiency and comfort. Theodore Winthrop, although he did not like the tents, is enthusiastic, as usual.

> Our tents are pitched on a level clover field sloping to the front of our parade ground. We use the old wall tent without a fly. It is necessary to live in one of these awhile

to know the vast superiority of the Sibley pattern. Sibley's tent is a wrinkle taken from savage life. It is the Sioux buffalo-skin lodge, or *Tepee*, improved,—a cone truncated at the top and fitted with a movable apex for ventilation. A single tent-pole, supported upon a hinged tripod of iron, sustains the structure. It is compacter, more commodious, healthier, and handsomer than the ancient models. None other should be used in permanent encampments. For marching troops, the French *Tente d'abri* is a capital shelter.

Still our fellows manage to be at home as they are. Some of our model tents are types of the best style of temporary cottages. Young housekeepers of limited incomes would do well to visit and take heed. A whole elysium of household comfort can be had out of a teapot,—tin; a brace of cups,—tin; a brace of plates,—tin; and a frying-pan.

In these days of war everybody can see a camp. Every one who stays at home has a brother or a son or a lover quartered in one of the myriad tents that have blossomed with the daffodil-season all over our green fields of the North. I need not, then, describe our encampment in detail,—its guard-tent in advance,—its guns in battery,—its flagstaff,—its companies quartered in streets with droll and fanciful names,—its officers' tents in the rear, at right angles to the lines of company-tents,—its kitchens, armed with Captain Viele's capital army cooking-stoves,—its big marquees, "The White House" and "Fort Pickens," for the lodging and messing of the new artillery company,—its barbers' shops,—its offices. The same, more or less well arranged can be seen in all the rendezvous where the armies are now assembling.[5]

The mansion itself was admirably suited for a head-quarters building, while the cellars, outbuildings, and greenhouse were capable of housing the commissary stores and the enormous quantity of food sent from New York by friends of the Regiment. A contemporary letter to one of the New York newspapers, dated May 16, describes the house.

On the right are the Colonel's and Quartermaster's quarters, plainly furnished, but comfortable. These are the best parlors, where Madison and Adams used to entertain their guests. On the left are the quarters of the Lieutenant-Colonel, Adjutant, and Major, their swords and other weapons hanging on the walls; tables covered with papers, a few chairs, and camp-stools making up the furniture. An intricate passage leads you into the rear, and, passing down a few steps, you find yourself in store-rooms of various kinds, the bakery, the Quartermaster's department, and various oval departments, where the members of the Engineer Corps have taken up their quarters, some stretched on mattresses, others busy with their arms and uniforms. Returning to the first floor, you ascend bridge-shaped stairs, and are on the second floor, where the officers and non-commissioned officers of engineers have their quarters. The rooms are small, but high of ceiling and airy, and were formerly used for bedrooms. Each room is occupied by six or eight men, according to size, and called by some familiar name. One was "Bleak House," another "Snug Home," and a third, I think, "Muggins." [6]

The visitor, who wrote the above description, is slightly inaccurate in locating a lieutenant-colonel's room. At the time the Regiment was lacking a lieutenant-colonel. He also appears confused in assigning so many rooms to the officers of the Tenth Company. Probably these quarters were assigned to the enlisted men.

Life at Camp Cameron now settled down to a pleasant routine for the next few weeks, and, except for the grim prospect of a nation at war, might have been just another annual encampment. Winthrop has left a delightful description of a typical day.

Boom! I would rather not believe it; but it is—yes it is—the morning gun, uttering its surly "Hullo!" to sunrise.

Yes,—and, to confirm my suspicions, here rattle in the drums and pipe in the fifes, wooing us to get up, *get up*, with music too peremptory to be harmonious.

I rise up *sur mon séant* and glance about me. I, Private W., chance, by reason of sundry chance, to be a member of a company recently largely recruited and bestowed all together in a big marquee. As I lift myself up, I see others lift themselves up on those straw bags we kindly call our mattresses. The tallest man of the regiment, Sergeant K., is on one side of me. On the other side I am separated from two of the fattest men of the regiment by Sergeant M., another excellent fellow, prime cook and prime forager.

We are all presently on our pins,—K. on those lengthy continuations of his, and the two stout gentlemen on their stout supporters. The deep sleepers are pulled up from those abysses of slumber where they had been choking, gurgling, strangling, death-rattling all night. There is for a moment a sound of legs rushing into pantaloons and arms plunging into jackets.

Then, as the drums and fifes whine and clatter their last notes, at the flap of our tents appears our orderly, and fierce in the morning sunshine gleams his moustache,—one month's growth this blessed day. "Fall in, for roll-call!" he cries, in a ringing voice. The orderly can speak sharp, if need be.

We obey. Not "Walk in!" "March in!" "Stand in!" is the order; but "Fall in!" as sleepy men must. Then the orderly calls off our hundred. There are several boyish voices which reply, several comic voices, a few mean voices, and some so earnest and manly and alert that one says to himself, "Those are the men for me, when work is to be done!" I read the character of my comrades every morning in each fellow's monosyllable "Here!"

When the orderly is satisfied that not one of us has run away and accepted a Colonelcy from the Confederate States since last roll-call, he notifies those unfortunates who are to be on guard for the next twenty-four hours of the honor and responsibility placed upon their shoulders. Next he tells us what are to be the drills of the day. Then "Right face! Dismissed! Break ranks! March!"

With ardor we instantly seize tin basins, soap, and towels, and invade a lovely oak-grove at the rear and left of our camp. Here is a delicious spring into which we have fitted a pump. The sylvan scene becomes peopled with "National Guards Washing,"—a scene meriting the notice of Art as much as any "Diana and her Nymphs." But we have no Poussin to paint us in the dewy sunlit grove. Few of us, indeed, know how picturesque we are at all times and seasons.

After this *beau ideal* of a morning toilet comes the ante-prandial drill. Lieutenant W. arrives, and gives us a little appetizing exercise in "Carry arms!" "Support arms!" "By the right flank, march!" "Double quick!"

Breakfast follows. My company messes somewhat helter-skelter in a big tent. We have very tolerable rations. Sometimes luxuries appear of potted meats and hermetical vegetables, sent us by the fond New Yorkers. Each little knot of fellows, too, cooks something savory. Our table-furniture is not elegant, our plates are tin, there is no silver in our forks; but *à la guerre, comme à la guerre.* Let the scrubs growl! Lucky fellows, if they suffer no worse hardships than this!

By-and-by, after breakfast, come company drills, bayonet practice, battalion drills, and the heavy work of the day. Our handsome Colonel, on a nice black nag, manoeuvres his thousand men of the line-companies on the parade for two or three hours. Two thousand legs step off accurately

together. Two thousand pipe-clayed cross belts—whitened
with infinite pains and waste of time, and offering a most
inviting mark to a foe—restrain the beating bosoms of a
thousand braves, as they—the braves, not the belts—go
through the most intricate evolutions unerringly. Watching
these battalion movements, Private W., perhaps, goes off
and inscribes in his journal,—"Any clever, prompt man,
with a mechanical turn, an eye for distance, a notion of
time, and a voice of command, can be a tactician. It is pure
pedantry to claim that the manoeuvring of troops is difficult: it is not difficult, if the troops are quick and steady.
But to be a general, with patience and purpose and initiative,—ah!" thinks Private W., "for that you must have
the man of genius; and already in this war he begins to
appear out of Massachusetts and elsewhere."

Private W. avows without fear that about noon, at Camp
Cameron, he takes a hearty dinner, and with satisfaction.
Private W. has had his feasts in cot and chateau in Old
World and New. It is the conviction of said private that
no-where and no-when has he expected his ration with more
interest, and remembered it with more affection, than here.

In the middle hours of the day it is in order to get a pass
to go to Washington, or visit some of the camps, which
now, in the middle of May, begin to form a cordon around
the city. Some of these I may criticize before the end of
this paper. Our capital seems arranged by Nature to be
protected by fortified camps on the circuit of its hills. It
may be made almost a Verona, if need be. Our brother
regiments have posts nearly as charming as our own in these
fair groves and on these fair slopes on either side of us.

In the afternoon comes target-practice, skirmishing-drill,
more company- or recruit-drill, and, at half-past five, our
evening parade. Let me not forget tent-inspection, at four,
by the officer of the day, when our band plays deliciously.

At evening parade all Washington appears. A regiment
of ladies, rather indisposed to beauty, observe us. Some-

times the Dons arrive,—Secretaries of State, of War, of Navy,—or military Dons, bestriding prancing steeds, but bestriding them as if "twas not their habit often of an afternoon." All which,—the bad teeth, pallid skins, and rustic toilets of the fair, and the very moderate horsemanship of the brave,—privates, standing at ease in the ranks, take note of, not cynically, but as men of the world.

Wondrous gymnasts are some of the Seventh, and after evening parade they often give exhibitions of their prowess to circles of admirers. Muscle has not gone out, nor nerve, nor activity, if these athletes are to be taken as the types or even as the leaders of the young city-bred men of our time. All the feats of strength and grace of the gymnasiums are to be seen here, and show to double advantage in the open air.

Then comes sweet evening. The moon rises. It seems always full moon at Camp Cameron. Every tent becomes a little illuminated pyramid. Cooking-fires burn bright along the alleys. The boys lark, sing, shout, do all those merry things that make the entertainment of volunteer service. The gentle moon looks on, mild and amused, the fairest lady of all that visit us.

At last when the songs have been sung and the hundred rumors of the day discussed, at ten the intrusive drums and scolding fifes get together and stir up a concert, always premature, called tattoo. The Seventh Regiment begins to peel for bed: at all events, Private W. does; for said W. takes, when he can, precious good care of his cuticle, and never yields to the lazy and unwholesome habit of soldiers, sleeping in the clothes. At taps—half-past ten—out go the lights. If they do not, presently comes the sentry's peremptory command to put them out. Then, and until the dawn of another day, a cordon of snorers inside of a cordon of sentries surrounds our national capital. The outer cordon sounds its "All's well"; and the inner cordon, slumbering, echoes it.

And that is the history of any day at Camp Cameron. It is monotonous, it is laborious, it is lazy, it is a bore, it is a lark, it is half-war, half-peace, and totally attractive and not to be dispensed with from one's experience in the nineteenth century.[7]

By now many of the regiments had received their equipment and a vast semi-circle of encampments sprang up on the hills surrounding Washington. Colonel Corcoran's Sixty-Nine New York was out on the grounds of Georgetown College, where the Jesuit fathers received them graciously. The New Jersey Brigade camped on Meridian Hill near the Seventh New York. The First and Second Connecticut marched out to W. W. Corcoran's estate at Glenwood. Their neighbors were the Rhode Island Regiment who camped near the cemetery. At the Navy Yard the Seventy-First New York stood guard. The city itself had been turned into a noisy, confused garrison, where it was almost impossible to move about without running into drilling troops. Ellsworth's Fire Zouaves, from New York, were all over the place, in a welter of pranks and general riot, much to the consternation of the sedate Washingtonians. The National Capital had been relieved with a vengeance.[8]

The center of attraction, however, was Camp Cameron, where the famous Seventh was busy proving itself the model regiment of the Union. There was no problem of discipline here, where each member of the Regiment had been thoroughly indoctrinated with the unit's sense of neatness, order, and regard for property. The evening dress parades were popular, and almost every afternoon the Fourteenth Street road was lined with carriages and horsemen on the way out to Meridian Hill. On May 7 the Regiment was reviewed by General Mansfield. With him was Major

Anderson, who was received enthusiastically by the companies he visited. On the following day Simon Cameron came out to inspect the camp. President Lincoln appeared on the twelfth with the Secretaries of State and of the Treasury, and the French and Brazilian ministers; on the thirteenth he reviewed the Regiment; and on the fifteenth visited again with Secretary Seward, and several members of New York's Union Defense Committee. The climax in ceremony, however, came on May 23 when a beautiful silk flag was presented to the Regiment. The flag had been made by some sixty young ladies of New York, who were relatives of members of the Regiment. They had requested Frederick Prime, of Edgewood in Westchester County, to make arrangements for the presentation. President Lincoln was again present and was accompanied by Adjutant-General Thomas in a review of the Regiment. At the conclusion of the review, the Regiment was closed in mass and General Thomas in a patriotic address, presented the flag to Colonel Lefferts. Accompanying the flag was a book containing the autographs of the makers, among whom were the granddaughters of John Jay, Alexander Hamilton, and General Clarkson, aide to General Washington, and the daughter of Comfort Sands, who was the last surviving member of the Committee of Safety of the city during the American Revolution.

On May 9 Private J. Larrie Keese of the Eighth Company was killed by the accidental discharge of a musket. Keese was well-known and had many close friends in the Regiment. The loss was thus very deeply felt and a detail from the Eighth Company was ordered to accompany the body to Brooklyn. The funeral was held at Christ Church and the burial at Greenwood Cemetery.

During the stay at Camp Cameron Colonel Lefferts had

considerable difficulty in holding down the number of recruits that were being sent to him from New York. On the day after the arrival at Camp Cameron the consolidated morning report showed a total strength of 1034 officers and men, excluding the band. They had left New York on April 19 with 991. To these were added the detachment that arrived in Annapolis in the *Baltic* and the 175 men who came on the first trip of the *Daylight*. On April 29 Lefferts had written to New York that he could receive no more recruits, except forty or fifty for the Tenth Company. Back in New York, however, the Veterans and the newly organized National Guard Reserve were finding it difficult to hold the line on the numbers of men who were begging for admission to the Regiment. On May 13 a detachment of 68 recruits for the Ninth Company arrived in Washington, under command of Sergeant Tyng, bringing the regimental strength to 1156. By May 20 the consolidated report showed 1231 men, and it was later to reach a peak of 1270. Many of the applicants, on the bare chance of being accepted, traveled to Washington at their own expense, and most of them were bitterly disappointed when they had to be turned down. Meantime, L. W. Stevens, the new Colonel of the Regiment's National Guard Reserve, and Asher Taylor, adjutant, were carrying on a running battle with General Sandford, who was attempting to block the transportation of any more men for the Seventh. Both Stevens and Taylor, along with Paymaster Kemp, complained to Lefferts that Sandford was preventing them from sending the men for the Tenth Company. Finally, however, they managed to find space on the *Matanzas* for twelve dollars per man, and Sergeant Tyng's detachment was able to join the Regiment.

As for supplies, the Seventh soon found itself deluged

with gifts of clothing and food, including every luxurious item that could be found on the market. Over and above the supplies that arrived on the *Daylight*, every train that came into Washington carried a shipment for the Regiment. Finally, the Quartermaster had to telegraph the Adams Express Company in New York:

> Do advise our friends to stop sending things to us. We have no means of keeping them; besides we are surfeited. Hereafter, demand prepayment on anything sent to us, except letters and articles of dress, which please send free.[9]

This message had little effect, however, for two weeks later one of the Philadelphia newspapers reported that, "on the 22d, the regiment received between eight and nine hundred boxes, bales, and packages from New York, containing supplies, donations, gifts, etc., and embracing all the luxuries the market could afford.[10] Some gifts were welcome. On May 11, one thousand havelocks reached the Regiment, the gift of the Ladies' Havelock Association of New York. These were the white linen cap-covers, designed by Sir Henry Havelock for the British troops in India, which were said to provide remarkable protection against the sun and were becoming most popular among all the regiments in Washington. Another gift was a supply of loose, dark gray, knit worsted jackets, donated by Mr. W. H. Aspinwall. They were immediately christened "Aspinwalls" by the men who welcomed them because, by this time, they were somewhat unhappy about the tight dress-coats, cross-belts, and pantaloons.

The Regiment also received, at this time, two twelve-pounder howitzers, the gift of Rutherford Stuyvesant, a member of the Regiment, who was unable to be with them. Accompanying the gift was the following letter:

175 Second Avenue, New York, May 3, 1861.

Marshall Lefferts, Colonel Seventh Regiment, N.Y.S.M.

Sir,—Being deprived, by ill health, of the great pleasure of sharing in the dangers and fatigues so well endured, and in the credit, so well merited, of the Seventh, I desire to testify my admiration for them as soldiers, and my affection for them as comrades, as well as my devotion to the sacred cause for which they are armed. With this intent, I have procured and forwarded to your address a pair of mounted howitzers, with their equipment and ammunition, which I desire to present to the regiment, with my best wishes.

I am, very respectfully yours, &c.,

Rutherford Stuyvesant.

The Seventh, however, almost lost them to the Thirteenth New York, as General Sandford reports in his letter of May 9 to Lefferts:

I sent the two howitzers presented to your regiment under the care of Brigade-Major Smith (1st Brigade) to Annapolis.

I have just seen a letter from Major Smith to General Spicer, asking him to inform me that Colonel Abel Smith, commanding the Thirteenth Regiment, had taken possession of these howitzers and declined to forward them, saying he needed them at Annapolis.

I have written to Colonel Smith to-day to say that he must send them to you at once. If there is any delay in so doing, please inform me.

I have a general order not to forward recruits, but I have taken the responsibility of sending forty for these howitzers to-day by the Empire City.[11]

Lefferts also received, about this time, two more rifled twelve-pounders, through the efforts of John Jacob Astor and the Union Defense Committee. These pieces were received, together with four hundred rounds of shot, four hundred of shell, eight hundred cartridges, and twelve hundred caps.

On May 3 President Lincoln, convinced now that the insurrection could not be crushed quickly, assumed full war powers and issued a proclamation calling into service 42,000 volunteers to serve for a period of three years. Within a few days the Seventh began to feel the effect of this proclamation, as various members resigned to accept commissions in other regiments. Among the first to leave was Noah L. Farnham, first lieutenant of the Second Company, who accepted the post of lieutenant-colonel in Ellsworth's Regiment of Fire Zouaves. Schuyler Hamilton, who had served as aide-de-camp to General Scott during the Mexican War, was appointed military secretary to the General on May 9, with the rank of lieutenant-colonel. He had left New York as a private in the Sixth Company, but had been acting as aide to General Butler since the Regiment landed in Annapolis. Several others accepted commissions in the Regular Army, and it soon became clear that the Seventh would be losing its best men. One of the letters from the Regiment, dated May 21, reports: "Five men from a single company, only one above the position of private, and he a sergeant, have received commissions in one regiment alone,—three of them the rank of captain. One brigadier commandant wants twelve captains from the Seventh." [12]

The proclamation also provoked a fundamental debate among the members of the Seventh concerning the future of the Regiment in the war. It was evident to all that the Regiment, as then constituted could not remain in service longer than for the brief period for which they had been mustered. Unlike most of the units now being mobilized, the Seventh had left with their regular complement of members and very few recruits. The men had simply dropped all their civilian concerns and marched off to Washington. No one had stopped to settle his business affairs or make arrangements for the support of his family. In return for this the Government had agreed to hold them in service for thirty days only. Most other regiments had recruited immediately, mostly from the unemployed, and the three months period imposed no particular hardship. On the other hand, many men of the Seventh were eager to serve for the duration of the war. Some were ready to remain in service; others wanted to hurry back to New York, settle their personal affairs, and sign up again. Most of those who had been in the Regiment for some time held a deep affection for the Seventh and wanted to see it remain in the field under its own colors for the duration. Thus, Major Shaler, Captain Clark, and a few others, proposed that those officers and members who wished to enlist for the war should reorganize the Regiment for the field, while those who were unable or unwilling to enlist should return to New York when their term of service expired. Their places could be filled by enlistments of qualified men, and the Regiment thus achieve the glory of fighting under its own banners. Colonel Lefferts opposed this strenuously. He was afraid of anything "that would endanger the identity and individuality of the Seventh Regiment, or weaken its position as a part of the militia of New York, and his unfortunate position upon this subject must ever be regarded as the great mistake of his military career." [13] Thus it was decided that the Regiment should return to New York when honorably discharged by the War Department, where each individual member could decide for himself how best to serve his country. Clark's plan probably would not have worked anyway. Most of the men were officer material, and it is most unlikely that their loyalty to the Seventh would prevent them from accepting commissions in other regiments.

IX Movement into Virginia

IT HAD long been evident to the War Department that the defense of Washington comprised more than filling up the city with volunteer militia. As early as May 3, Colonel Mansfield, who was an engineer, had drawn up plans, recommending to General Scott that Arlington Heights be occupied. In his letter of that date he states:

> . . . Here I must remark that the President's House and Department buildings in its vicinity are but two and a half miles across the river from Arlington high ground, where a battery of bombs and heavy guns, if established, could destroy the city with comparatively a small force after destroying the bridges. The Capitol is only three and a half miles from the same height at Arlington, and at the Aqueduct the summits of the heights on the opposite shore are not over one mile from Georgetown.
>
> With this view of the condition of our position, it is clear to my mind that the city is liable to be bombarded at the will of an enemy, unless we occupy the ground which he certainly would occupy if he had any such intention. I therefore recommend that the heights above mentioned be seized and secured by at least two strong redoubts, one commanding the Long Bridge and the other the Aqueduct, and that a body of men be there encamped to sustain the

redoubts and give battle to the enemy if necessary. I have engineers maturing plans and reconnoitering further. It is quite probable that our troops assembled in Arlington would create much excitement in Virginia, yet, at the same time, if the enemy were to occupy the ground there a greater excitement would take place on our side, and it might be necessary to fight a battle to disadvantage.[1]

Scott agreed completely, but the actual advance could not be ordered until the Virginia vote on the ordinance of secession. The ordinance, adopted by the State Convention on April 17, 1861, provided that it should take effect when ratified by a majority of the votes of the people of the state. The date set for voting was the fourth Thursday of May, the twenty-third. Although it was a foregone conclusion that the people would ratify the ordinance, Lincoln was powerless under the Constitution to send Federal troops into Virginia until an insurrection existed legally. Nevertheless, preparations had to be made, and Mansfield was allowed to draw up a plan of operations.

The expedition was to be a major movement, involving eleven regiments together with assorted companies of cavalry, artillery, and pioneers. Captain W. H. Wood, Third United States Infantry, was placed in command of the column ordered to cross the Aqueduct at Georgetown. His command consisted of the Fifth, Twenty-Eighth, and Sixty-Ninth New York Regiments, one company of cavalry, one section of artillery, and forty-eight pioneers of the Fourteenth New York. Colonel S. P. Heintzelman, who was at that time acting Inspector-General for Mansfield, commanded the troops crossing the Long Bridge. With him were the Seventh, Twelfth, and Twenty-Fifth New York Regiments, the First Michigan, and the New Jersey Brigade, consisting of three regiments under Gen. Theodore Runyon. His force also included two companies of cavalry and two sections of artillery. Colonel Ellsworth's Fire Zouaves, who had finally gone into camp along the Potomac, much to the relief of the citizens of Washington, were ordered to cross the river by boat and land at Alexandria.[2] The main purpose of the movement was to ensure the safety of the Capital by occupying nearby Virginia territory and building there a series of forts. It is unlikely that Scott and Mansfield expected much opposition, although they were probably aware that some Virginia troops had moved back into Alexandria. Lieutenant-Colonel A. S. Taylor, commanding the Virginia Volunteers at Alexandria, had brought down a considerable storm about his head by evacuating the town on May 5. In his report he explained that he had retired from Alexandria because "of the inefficient condition of a large proportion of the troops and my exposed and indefensible position"; that his "men were becoming almost useless from home influences"; and, futhermore, that he "was possessed of, apparently, such reliable information that the Government at Washington would occupy Alexandria on the 6th or 7th instant." [3] Gen. Philip Cocke, commanding the Department of the Potomac, almost had him arrested for this maneuver but in the end deferred to General Robert E. Lee's intervention in Taylor's behalf. By the twenty-third Col. George H. Terrett had been ordered back into Alexandria with five hundred Virginia infantry.

Colonel Heintzelman and Captain Wood evidently had a delicate command problem on their hands in carrying out the operation. Mansfield obviously felt that he could trust only Regular Army officers with this assignment despite the fact that he had two generals of state troops on his hands. In addition to General Runyon, General Charles W.

Sandford had come down from New York to lead his regiments in Washington. Fortunately the two Army officers handled the matter diplomatically, and Sandford, at least, finished the operation, convinced that he had been in command all along.

Out at Camp Cameron the Seventh Regiment received the following orders on the afternoon of May 23:

> Head-quarters, Department Washington
> May 23, 1861.
>
> Colonel Lefferts, New York Seventh Infantry.
>
> Sir,—Please have your regiment at the head of Long Bridge by two o'clock to-night, and let them march without music or noise, and report to Colonel Heintzelman, United States Army.
>
> Mansfield, B.G. & Commanding[4]

Immediately after the flag presentation ceremony the company commanders broke the news to the men who were generally bored with the lazy camp life and were delighted that something new was going to happen. As Winthrop describes the scene:

> Something in the wind! As I was strolling off to see the sunset and the ladies on parade, I began to hear great irrepressible cheers bursting from the streets of the different companies.
>
> "Orders to be ready to march at a moment's notice!"— So I learned presently from dozens of overjoyed fellows. "Harper's Ferry!" says one. "Alexandria!" shouts a second. "Richmond!" only Richmond will content a third. And some could hardly be satisfied short of the hope of a breakfast in Montgomery.
>
> What a happy thousand were the line companies! How their suppressed ardors stirred! No want of fight in these lads! They may be rather luxurious in their habits,

for camp life. They may be a little impatient of restraint. They may have—as the type regiment of militia—the type faults of militia on service. But a desire to dodge a fight is not one of these faults.[5]

There were some unhappy faces in the crowd, however. The two artillery companies, the Ninth and Tenth, were ordered to remain behind to guard the camp. At eleven P.M. Colonel Lefferts issued the following instructions to Capt. George C. Farrar, Tenth Company:

> Sir,—You will immediately parade your company, and relieve from further duty the present camp-guard. As soon as the regiment leaves the ground, all persons except those in uniform must be excluded from the camp-ground. Any friends wishing to see members of the regiment can do so at the Colonel's head-quarters. There is a large amount of property in camp, and you must exercise the utmost vigilance and care. You will have one prisoner in the camp-ground. He is to be held until further notice.[6]

Private Winthrop, who could lay claim to the status of journalist—he had probably been commissioned by *Atlantic Monthly* to write a series of articles—managed to get himself transferred to the Eighth Company so that he could report the march.

At one A.M., May 24, the companies formed in line and the column filed noiselessly through the camp to the highway. No one seems to have informed the drummers of the direction of the Regiment, and, inevitably, they made the wrong turn and started up the road away from Washington. Colonel Lefferts, at this point, hurried forward and moved them in the opposite direction. The Seventh then knew that it was going, not to Harpers Ferry as had been rumored, but to Alexandria, or for the more exuberant, Richmond. The route took them down Fourteenth Street, across Pennsylvania Avenue at Willard's Hotel, and then on to the new Washington Monument where they halted. The orders were for the Twelfth New York to lead the way across Long Bridge at two A.M., followed by the Twenty-Fifth New York and the New Jersey Brigade. The Seventh was ordered to move across the bridge and halt a short distance beyond it in order to hold the bridge-head. Winthrop tells the story of the march:

> So we pegged along to Washington and across Washington,—which at that point consists of Willard's Hotel, few other buildings being in sight. A hag in a nightcap reviewed us from an upper window as we tramped by.
>
> Opposite that bald block, the Washington Monument, and opposite what was more important to us, a drove of beeves putting beef on their bones in the seedy grounds of the Smithsonian Institution, we were halted while the New Jersey brigade—some three thousand of them— trudged by, receiving the complimentary fire of our line as they passed. New Jersey is not so far from New York but that the dialects of the two can understand each other. Their respective slangs, though peculiar, are of the same genus. By the end of this war, I trust that these distinctions of locality will be quite annulled.
>
> We began to feel like an army as these thousands thronged by us. This was evidently a movement in force. We rested an hour or more by the road. Mounted officers galloping along down the lines kept up the excitement.
>
> At last we had the word to fall in again and march. It is part of the simple perfection of the machine, a regiment, that, though it drops to pieces for a rest, it comes together instantly for a start, and nobody is confused or delayed. We moved half a mile farther, and presently a broad pathway of reflected moonlight shone up at us from the Potomac. . . .

The Long Bridge thus far has been merely a shabby causeway with waterways and draws. Shabby,—let me here pause to say that in Virginia shabbiness is the grand universal law, and neatness the spasmodic exception, attained in rare spots, an aeon beyond their old Dominion.

The Long Bridge has thus far been a totally unhistoric and prosaic bridge. Roads and bridges are making themselves of importance and shining up into sudden renown in these times. The Long Bridge has done nothing hitherto except carry passengers on its back across the Potomac. Hucksters, planters, dry-goods drummers, Members of Congress, *et ea genera omnia,* have here gone and come on their several mercenary errands, and, as it now appears, some sour little imp—the very reverse of a "sweet little cherub"—took toll of every man as he passed,— a heavy toll, namely, every man's whole store of Patriotism and Loyalty. Every man—so it seems—who passed the Long Bridge was stripped of his last dollar of *Amor Patriae,* and came to Washington, or went home, with a waistcoat-pocket full of bogus in change. It was our business now to open the bridge and see it clear, and leave sentries along to keep it permanently free for Freedom.

There is a mile of this Long Bridge. We seemed to occupy the whole length of it, with our files opened to diffuse the weight of our column. We were not now the tired and sleepy squad which just a moon ago had trudged along the railroad to the Annapolis Junction, looking up a Capital and a Government, perhaps lost.

By the time we touched ground across the bridge, dawn was breaking,—a good omen for poor old sleepy Virginia. The moon, as bright and handsome as a new twenty-dollar piece, carried herself straight before us,—a splendid oriflamme.

Lucky is the private who marches with the van! It may be the post of more danger, but it is also the post of less dust. My throat, therefore, and my eyes and beard, wore the

less Southern soil when we halted half a mile beyond the
bridge, and let sunrise overtake us.[7]

The Regiment halted at four A.M., a half-mile beyond
the Potomac, their first bivouac in Virginia. "A picturesque
bivouac it was. The sleepy dropped on the railway track and
slept soundly. The active organized into impromptu foraging parties, laid hold on neighboring fence-rails and soon
had fires flaming in the air, and raw pork and ham sizzling
and frying in better or worse cookery." [8] When daylight
came, the New Jersey troops could be seen ahead busily
digging entrenchments. Mounted couriers and orderlies
dashed back and forth across Long Bridge. In the middle
of the morning one of them stopped long enough to shout
out that Alexandria had been taken, but that Ellsworth had
been killed. The news was shattering. Ellsworth was a favorite of all, particularly the Seventh Regiment, who remembered fondly the visit of his Chicago Zouaves to New York
in 1860. The capture of Alexandria had gone according to
plan. The Fire Zouaves were landed there under protection
of the guns of the *Pawnee,* and were then joined by the
First Michigan, which had marched across Long Bridge.
Ellsworth, impetuous as always, went himself to the roof of
the Marshall House and tore down the Confederate flag. On
his way down the stairs the inn-keeper appeared and shot
him through the heart. He was succeeded in command by
the Seventh Regiment officer, Col. Noah L. Farnham.

As the day progressed the heat became intense, and the
Regiment was ordered off the dusty road into the grounds
of an adjoining race-course. From there, the monotonous
task of covering Long Bridge and waiting for any call for
reserves could be accomplished adequately—and much
more comfortably. At six P.M. orders came to move into a
cedar grove near Columbia Spring on the grounds of the

Arlington estate, which was then occupied by the Lee family. Once again, the Seventh had snagged the choicest camp-site. "The grounds were neatly sodded, clean and dry. Beautiful trees of nearly every variety indigenous to Virginia, although evergreens were most numerous, adorned the lawn, and completely shut out the sun, the sky, and the surrounding world. An inexhaustible spring of crystal water was near at hand, and the forest furnished green boughs for rustic habitations and wood for fuel." [9]

Colonel Lefferts was reluctant to continue his men in idleness and at daylight on the morning of Saturday, May 25, ordered Captain Viele to try to arrange for the Seventh to help in the construction of the redoubt, which was to be called Fort Runyon. The engineer officer in charge was delighted with the offer. In a short time the Seventh was therefore detailed to dig trenches on two-hour shifts. General Sandford meanwhile had the same idea as Lefferts and issued the following orders at ten A.M.

> Colonel Lefferts will detail a working party from his regiment for duty in the trenches, this morning. His regiment will be relieved by one of the Massachusetts regiments detailed by General Mansfield, upon the arrival of which the Seventh will return to the camp in Washington City, and wait further orders.

At ten A.M. Lefferts sent the following reply:

> Sir,—Special order of this date just received. I sent Captain Viele at daylight this morning to the trenches, asking of the engineer in command, as a special favor, that he would allow my men to go to work and relieve the New Jersey regiment. He consented for us to throw up a new line marked out, and they are now at work, thus anticipating so much of your order. [10]

Hard work it was, and the effete members of the Seventh pitched in enthusiastically all through Saturday and Sunday, acquiring a phenomenal number of blisters and sore muscles. Even Chaplain Weston, when he finished divine service on Sunday, laid down his Bible and manned a shovel for two hours. Private Winthrop was delighted with his own contribution.

This was my first view of a field-work in construction,—also, my first hand as a laborer at a field-work. I knew glacis and counterscarp on paper; also, on paper, superior slope, banquette, and the other dirty parts of a redoubt. Here they were, not on paper. A slight wooden scaffolding determined the shape of the simple work; and when I arrived, a thousand Jerseymen, with picks, spades, and shovels, cutting into Virginia, shovelling up Virginia, for Virginia's protection against pseudo-Virginians.

I swarmed in for a little while with our Paymaster, picked a little, spaded a little, took a hand to my great satisfaction at earth-works, and for my efforts I venture to suggest that Jersey City owes me its freedom in a box, and Jersey State a basket of its finest Clicquot.[11]

Late in the afternoon of Sunday, May 26, however, the labor came to an end upon receipt of the following orders:

Headquarters, Department of Washington,
Sunday, May 26, 1861.

Colonel Lefferts, Commanding Seventh Regiment of New York:

Sir,—Your regiment has accomplished all that was intended in coming over to Arlington to take possession of the Heights, and has labored very manfully in the intrenchments also. The security of this city (Washington) renders it imperative that you should resume your encampment, and you will this afternoon march over accordingly,

and hold your regiment ready to turn out when called upon.
Very respectfully,
J. K. F. Mansfield,
General Commanding Department of
Washington.[12]

At sundown the Seventh left Virginia, crossed Long
Bridge in a drenching rainstorm, and tramped through the
mud up Fourteenth Street to Camp Cameron where the
Ninth and Tenth Companies lined up with the band to
receive them. One of the men in a letter recalls: "One hand
holding pieces at 'present arms,' the other waving caps,
shaking hands, or welcoming by a slap on the shoulders the
men as they passed the guard-tent; the band on the right
of the guard playing 'Home Again,' while to this music
was added the ringing cheers of the glad fellows who had
so reluctantly remained at home while we 'went to the
wars.' " [13]

It was now time to go home. The Regiment had been
mustered in for thirty days and the time had now expired.
The War Department, however, was reluctant to discharge
them and asked Lefferts to wait at least a few days longer.
Thus, on May 28 the Colonel addressed the Regiment,
informing them that the Government was still in want of
their services and that he hoped they would consent to
stay as long as they were needed. He pointed out that the
Government had informed him that the additional service
would be only for a few days. He offered furloughs to any
who wanted them, but only five applied. The Regiment
then unanimously agreed to remain as long as the Government needed their services.

Unanimous votes on the parade ground were all fine,
but it soon became evident that a majority of the Regiment

wanted a return to New York as soon as possible. As Swinton explains:

> That it could have been otherwise will hardly be imagined by any one who for a moment considers the circumstances under which the National Guard so suddenly started to Washington. Families had been left unprovided for; extensive businesses had been dropped, and, in the general derangement of finance, were going to ruin; commercial positions had been sacrificed, and the call of the country had alone been heard.[14]

As evidence of this sentiment Colonel Lefferts received the following note from one of his officers a few hours after he had addressed the Regiment:

> I have had a personal interview with every member of our company now in camp. There is perfect unanimity of sentiment, and that is to stay two or three days longer.
>
> The sentiment is equally unanimous not to stay beyond Saturday at the latest. The members of this company are unanimous in saying that they will be obliged to go on that day, if not before relieved. I hope you will be able to make arrangements so that this company, which has so nobly responded to your request, may go home at that time with honor, and before that time if possible. I wish you distinctly to understand, that this unanimity has been obtained upon your assurance that we are to go home by Saturday next, at the latest.[15]

In the light of these circumstances Lefferts had no choice but to exert whatever pressure he could on the War Department to speed up the discharge orders. He succeeded, and on May 30 Secretary Cameron came out to address the Seventh, thanking them effusively on behalf of the Government. He then announced that the order has been issued for their return to New York, to be mustered out of service. The following is the text of the order:

War Department, Adjutant-General's Office
Washington, May 30, 1861

Special Order No. 146.

The commanding officer of the Seventh Regiment, New York militia, will proceed with his regiment to the city of New York, where it will be mustered out of the service of the United States by Lieutenant M. Cogswell, Eighth Infantry.

It is the desire of the War Department, in relinquishing the services of this gallant regiment, to make known the satisfaction that is felt at the prompt and patriotic manner in which it responded to the call for men to defend the Capital, when it was believed to have been in peril, and to acknowledge the important service it rendered, by appearing here in an hour of dark and trying necessity. The time for which it had engaged to serve has now expired; the service which it was expected to perform has been handsomely accomplished, and its members may return to their native city with the assurance that its services are gratefully appreciated by all good and loyal citizens, while the Government is equally confident that when the country again calls upon them, its appeal will not be made in vain to the young men of New York.

By order, L. Thomas, Adjutant-General.

To Colonel Lefferts,
Commanding Seventh Regiment, Camp Cameron.[16]

The news was received joyfully by the men, who wasted no time in breaking up the camp. That night, the band and a group of the men under Lieutenant Bostwick marched into Washington and serenaded the President at the White House. They then moved on to Secretary Seward's home and then to Willard's Hotel to pay tribute to Major McDowell and General Mansfield. The next day, arrangements for departure were continued. The camp equipage was sold to the Government, while the camp furniture, fixtures, utensils, provisions, etc. were left as a gift for the Ninth New York Volunteers. As a final gesture a collection was taken among the members of the Regiment, and as a result $103.00 was contributed for the completion of the Washington Monument.

At 3:30 P.M. on May 31, the Seventh left Camp Cameron and marched to the railway depot. Not without a last minute display of temperament, however. Just before they left, General Sandford had sent the following message to Lefferts:

> I have just received intelligence, through the highest military sources, that there was a collision yesterday on Federal Hill, Baltimore, between the pickets of our troops and some of the Baltimore rowdies, in which three of the latter were shot. A great excitement prevails there, and I am advised that it is imprudent to let the Seventh go through Baltimore at night. This opinion is from the highest sources. I deem it my duty, therefore (whilst I omit to issue an order), to advise you to defer your departure until an early hour to-morrow morning.[17]

In the morning he had also received a telegram from W. Prescott Smith, of the Baltimore and Ohio Railroad.

> Our agent at Washington telegraphs me that you stated you would march your regiment through Baltimore. Permit me to advise you, that, by direction of the Railway Officers of the War Department to-day, we have arranged with Bay steamers and Philadephia road to transfer you at the harbor from the Locust Point station to Canton. This will obviate any march here, and greatly facilitate your movements.[18]

At this point Colonel Lefferts and his officers turned stubborn. For some undisclosed reason they resolved not to accept the change in railroad arrangements unless they received a peremptory order from the War Department. Accordingly at 6:15 P.M. Lefferts sent the following message to Smith:

> On the Train, May 31, 1861
>
> Your despatch received. Was it the order of the War Department to go to Locust Point? Does any cause exist why we should not march from depot to depot? I of course wish to obey instructions. Answer at Relay House.

Smith's answer follows:

> We were directed specifically from Washington, by the General Railway Managers for War Department, to arrange for your transfer at Locust Point. We have to do so, and to change it at this late hour would make delay and confusion. But for this, no cause would exist why you should not march from depot to depot as you prefer. The plan arranged is more expensive and troublesome to us, but will facilitate yours. We will take you to Locust Point accordingly.[19]

What Superintendent Smith failed to realize was that the Seventh, once it had decided on a particular course of action, was a most difficult organization to change. It is possible that the officers were concerned lest the impression go out to the press that they were anxious to avoid a collision with the mob in Baltimore. At any rate Lefferts appealed to Washington and received permission to use his own judgment. He therefore notified Smith that, "We prefer to march from depot to depot, as no reason exists why we should not." Arriving at Baltimore about eleven P.M., the Regiment marched through the city by the most direct route without interruption to the Camden Station, and embarked for Philadelphia. At ten A.M. June 1 they reached Philadelphia and marched down Prime Street to the Camden Ferry, thence to move on to New York.

Everyone was more or less concerned about the reception that might await them. There had been some criticism on the point of their early dismissal from service, inspired mostly by letters from other New York regiments, which were remaining in service for the full three months. The criticism, of course, overlooked the fact that the Seventh had marched without waiting to recruit new members, who were able to make suitable personal arrangements for a longer term of service. By the time the Regiment reached New York, however, most of the unfavorable comment had died down, particularly because the newspapers defended them vigorously and went out of their way to explain the situation.

At five P.M. the train reached Jersey City and the depot was just as crowded as it was on April 19. In Cortlandt Street they were formally received by the Veterans of the Seventh Regiment, a detachment of the Sickles Brigade, and by the Union Defense Committee. Again the nineteenth of April repeated itself, and the Seventh marched through dense, cheering crowds to the Armory, which had been decorated with flowers by the ladies of the Regiment. At the Armory the confusion was so great and the crowd so large that the Regiment had to be dismissed without ceremony. Mr. John Jacob Astor, however, was able to present the following resolution to Colonel Lefferts, on behalf of the Union Defense Committee:

> Resolved: That this Committee desires to express its cordial recognition of the efficient services rendered to the cause of the country at a critical emergency of its public

affairs by the Seventh Regiment, N.Y. Militia, commanded
by Colonel Marshall Lefferts, and sharing fully in the
general feeling of gratification which pervades this community at learning that the Commanding General of the
United States Army, under the sanction of the President
of the United States, has acknowledged, in special orders,
the important services rendered by that Regiment in an
hour of dark and trying necessity, the Committee desires
to unite their congratulations with those of their fellow-
citizens in extending a welcome hand to cheer the return
of a body of soldiers which has conferred such high honor
on the City of New York.

Resolved: That this Committee will take pleasure in
attending the reception to be given the Seventh Regiment.

Resolved: That these proceedings be published and a
copy furnished to Colonel Lefferts.

J. J. Astor, Jr., Chairman Executive Committee.
P. M. Wetmore, Secretary.[20]

On June 3 the Seventh was mustered out of the service
of the United States in accordance with Colonel Leffert's
final order of the campaign:

The Regiment will assemble at Head-Quarters on Monday, 3d instant, at half-past one o'clock, P.M., fully
equipped, for the purpose of being mustered out of the
service of the United States by Lieutenant M. Cogswell,
Eighth Infantry, U.S.A., who has been assigned that duty.

The Colonel takes this opportunity to express to the officers and soldiers his deep sense of the manly virtues and
patriotism which have actuated all in their discharge of
duty, from the time we received our marching orders for
the protection of the Federal Capital to the present time;
how far the objects of the mission have been accomplished,
and how well the duty has been performed, must be left

to the impartial judgment of the future. I congratulate you, brother soldiers, that it was our good fortune to lead the strong and noble army of our good and loyal State, which stands with poised arm to strike down all who may defy the power of the national ensign, which it has planted in the face of those who would trail its sacred folds in the dust.

Let it be understood that we are ready at a moment's warning to march at the call of the constituted authorities in defense of our flag and country.[21]

The Common Council of the city, not to be outdone in these encomiums, adopted the following resolution on June 3, which made a fitting climax for the forty-six days of service:

Whereas; The officers and members of the gallant Seventh Regiment, N.Y. Militia, noted for the alacrity with which they always respond to the calls of duty, after having nobly and successfully aided in accomplishing the task of opening the way to and protecting the Capital of the Nation whilst in immediate danger from armed traitors, who beleaguered it on every side, have just returned to our city, of which, both as a military organization and as distinguished and patriotic citizens, they have enjoyed a wide-spread reputation, which their soldierly demeanor, untiring vigilance, and unflagging energy in discharging the arduous duties from which they have just returned, prove them to have so well merited; be it, therefore,

Resolved: That the Common Council of the City of New York welcome them back with feelings of joy and gratitude to our city, which feels a just pride in them, both as citizens and as soldiers, and to their families and homes, which they have honored by their noble demeanor and now make happy by their presence.

Resolved: That the Clerk of Common Council have the foregoing resolutions suitably engrossed, and forward the same to the Regiment.

Adopted by the	Adopted by the	Approved by the
Board of Councilmen	Board of Aldermen	Mayor
June 3, 1861	June 7, 1861	June 8, 1861

D. T. Valentine, Clerk of Common Council.[22]

X Return to New York and Aftermath

THE FORTY-SIX DAYS had now really come to an end. It remained only for the Regiment to be paid, and on August 12 Paymaster Patten, U.S.A., who had previously been Commissary of the Seventh, handed each member a little over twenty dollars in gold coin. The Regiment would not be the same again for a long time to come. The membership quickly dropped below nine-hundred as more and more men accepted commissions in regiments scattered all over the Nation. This was going to be a long hard war, fought by the swelling volume of volunteer regiments enlisted for the duration. The Seventh had done its job by moving in quickly at the moment of danger. Now the second phase of its contribution was beginning as it fed its best men into the vast military machine that was building up in the North. They were called out again as a regiment in 1862, when Stonewall Jackson was driving the Union command to distraction by his brilliant Shenandoah Valley campaign. They saw service again in 1863, when Lee made his thrust into Pennsylvania, and they took a major part in quelling the New York draft riots. The big story, however, was in Virginia and out on the Mississippi, and, in the eyes of most, the Seventh had reverted to a

179

crack parade outfit and means of quelling local disorders.

The exodus started early, even before they left Washington. Schuyler Hamilton was the first one recorded, but he had been a member of the Seventh for only a short time. He had a long military background, and General Scott was anxious to use him as military secretary. Later, he became Assistant Chief of Staff to General Halleck. As a brigadier-general he performed brilliantly under Pope in the Army of the Mississippi and is credited with suggesting the cutting of the canal at Island Number Ten to turn the enemy's position. He had to refuse promotion to Major-General because he caught malaria and resigned on February 27, 1863.

In Farnham's case the feeling was different. Noah L. Farnham had a long association with the Seventh and was a most popular first lieutenant of the Second Company. When Ellsworth was killed at Alexandria, Farnham succeeded to the command of the Eleventh New York Volunteers (Fire Zouaves). His luck had run out, however. At Bull Run on July 18, 1861, he was struck on the side of the head by a musket-ball. He died from his wound on August 14.

The service record of the men of the Seventh is long and filled with outstanding exploits. Only a few can be recounted here. Of them all, Theodore Winthrop stands out, partly because he was the first to die on the battle-field, and partly because he had chronicled the doings of the Seventh so faithfully and so extravagantly. General Butler was delighted to get him as military secretary. The feeling was mutual, for Winthrop had succumbed completely to Butler's dynamic personality. He thought of him as a one-man army and recalls that when he arrived at Fort Monroe he found the "neighborhood occupied by two armies:

1. General Butler; 2. About six thousand men, here and at Newport's News." Winthrop was a popular novelist and essayist. His death at the battle of Great Bethel on June 10, 1861, produced a deep sensation of grief throughout the country. In his obituary in the *Atlantic Monthly* it is recalled:

> On the 19th of April he left the armory door of the Seventh, with his hand upon a howitzer; on the 21st of June his body lay upon the same howitzer at the same door, wrapped in the flag for which he gladly died, as the symbol of human freedom. And so, drawn by the hands of young men lately strangers to him, but of whose bravery and loyalty he had been the laureate, and who fitly mourned him who had honored them, with long pealing dirges and muffled drums, he moved forward.[1]

Fitz-James O'Brien's literary career was even more promising than that of Winthrop. He was becoming recognized as an important poet and dramatist and had contributed prolifically to *Harper's Weekly*. When the Seventh returned from Washington he was disappointed that it was not going to remain in active service. He resigned, therefore, and tried to recruit a volunteer regiment called the McClellan Rifles. General Frederick W. Lander, however, was looking for officers for his brigade in West Virginia, and O'Brien was one of five members of the Seventh who accepted commissions. On February 16, 1862, as captain in command of a body of cavalry, he exchanged shots with the leader of a Confederate force and was wounded severely in the shoulder. A critical operation was necessary, concerning which O'Brien wrote to a friend, probably William Winter:

> I gave up the ghost, and told him to go ahead. There were about twelve surgeons to witness the operation. All

my shoulder-bone and a portion of my upper arm have been taken away. I nearly died. My breath ceased, heart ceased to beat, pulse stopped. However, I got through. I am not yet out of danger from the operation, but a worse disease has set in. I have got tetanus, or lockjaw. There is a chance of my getting out of it, that's all. In case I don't, good-by, old fellow, with all my love! I don't want to make any legal document, but I desire that you and Frank Wood should be my literary executors, because after I'm dead I may turn out a bigger man than when living.[2]

His premonition was sound. He died on April 6, 1862.

To Private Robert G. Shaw, of the Sixth Company, came a unique honor. In 1863 he was Colonel of the Fifty-Fourth Massachusetts Volunteers, the first Negro regiment recruited under state authority. On July 19 of that year he led the famous storming column at the assault of Fort Wagner. One of the first to scale the walls, he was shot dead as he reached the top of the parapet. Alongside of him fell a negro color-sergeant. Brigadier-General Haygood, commanding the Confederate forces, said, "I knew Colonel Shaw before the war, and then esteemed him; had he been in command of white troops, I should have given him an honorable burial. As it is, I shall bury him in the common trench, with the Negroes that fell with him." [3]

The Seventh had three Congressional Medal of Honor winners in the Civil War. One of them was Major Alexander Shaler, who left the Regiment to help organize the Sixty-Fifth New York Volunteers, of which he became Lieutenant-Colonel. Shaler was known in the Seventh as an austere and brusque disciplinarian who would not tolerate even the slightest error in drill. In June, 1862, he was promoted to Colonel and served in all the battles of the Army of the Potomac until the fall of 1863. For his "gallantry and meritorious conduct" at Mary's Heights on May 3, 1862, he was awarded the Medal of Honor and promoted to Brigadier-General. Taken prisoner at the Battle of the Wilderness, he was held at Charleston from May to August, 1864. He was brevetted Major-General on July 27, 1865. The other medalists were Charles J. Murphy, private in the Fourth Company from 1852-59 and Charles M. Rockefeller, whom Emmons Clark lists as a member of the Fifth Company in the regimental muster of April, 1861. Murphy, first lieutenant of the Thirty-Eighth New York Volunteers was honored for his service at Bull Run in 1861; Rockefeller, lieutenant, 178th New York Volunteers, for services at Fort Blakely, Alabama, April 9, 1865.

Of the remaining officers of the Seventh in April-May 1861, Captain Egbert L. Viele, Adjutant J. Henry Liebenau, and Asst. Surg. John C. Dalton were commissioned in the United States Volunteers. Viele had been in the Regiment since 1859. He was a graduate of West Point who resigned his Regular Army commission in 1853 to become a civil engineer. He was appointed Brigadier-General, United States Volunteers, in August, 1861. His brigade took part in the Dupont Expedition at the capture of Port Royal. After the occupation of Norfolk he was appointed Military Governor of that city. In 1863 he resigned his commission. Subsequently, he was a Commissioner of Public Parks and Member of Congress from New York City. The other officers who served in the war were William Gurney, Richard F. Halsted, John D. Moriarty, William Patten, Edward Bernard, and Thomas B. Bunting. Of these, Gurney rose to the rank of Brigadier-General.

Marshall Lefferts continued on as Colonel of the Seventh until 1864. When the American Telegraph Company was formed in 1861 he joined it as electrical engineer. Under his direction the long lines were installed and vast improvements instituted in the system of detecting electrical failure and reducing the resistance of relays. When the company consolidated with the Western Union Telegraph Company in 1866, it was recognized as one of the most efficient telegraphic systems in the world. Despite this heavy schedule Lefferts was able to lead his regiment into active service again in 1862 and 1863. During the latter campaign he served for a time as Military Governor of Frederick, Maryland.

The choice of Emmons B. Clark as Colonel to succeed Marshall Lefferts on June 21, 1864 came as no surprise. He had done a superb job as Captain of the Second Company. His loyalty and devotion to the Regiment were outstanding. During the next twenty-five years he guided the destinies of the Seventh. In civilian life he was secretary of the New York City Health Department from 1866 to 1903. All his spare time, however, went into the Seventh Regiment. It was due principally to his efforts that the Seventh was carried over the difficult post-war years of military apathy, when so many of the city's military organizations went out of existence. Colonel Clark also originated the movement for a new armory as early as 1868. The opening of the building on Park Avenue in 1880 came about largely through his initiative, vision, and unquenchable energy.

In any assessment of the Seventh Regiment's true value to the Union in 1861 it is necessary to thread one's way carefully through the records of contemporary opinion. On the one hand there was, at the time, excessive adulation of the Regiment; on the other hand, there was unwarranted criticism. The Seventh New York was a superb regiment, probably the best militia organization in the country. Its discipline was tight, its drilling almost perfect, its *esprit de corps* of the highest order. Even allowing for the literary propensities of the period, the lavish praise and idolization heaped upon the Regiment was a bit too thick. Perhaps this had to be expected from the early historians of the Seventh. The same tone of extravagance was unwarranted in newspaper accounts, public speeches, and resolutions. How much of this adoration rubbed off on the members of the Regiment is difficult to say. It is unlikely that most of them took themselves that seriously. They had too intelligent a sense of humor for that. As for the criticism, much of it was petty military jealousy coming from less well-organized regiments. They disparaged with envious eyes the Seventh's striving for perfection and, unfortunately, wrote letters home about it. Another source of antagonism lay in the mere fact that they were the "silk stocking regiment." The Regiment was too wealthy, its members came from families that were too prominent socially, to avoid making enemies. They were still, and always would be, to some the "Old Greybacks" of 1849.

The achievement of the Seventh in 1861 does not rest primarily on the fact that Washington was saved, or in their part in the occupation of Arlington Heights. The Capital would have been relieved anyway, and the Seventh was only one of many in the occupation. They marched off promptly and willingly to Washington; spent far too much time getting there, partially through their own obstinacy and sensitivity; underwent a fairly laborious march to Annapolis Junction; set up a model encampment; dug the southwest angle of Fort Runyon.

The contribution of the Seventh Regiment has deeper roots than that. It was not just any regiment that relieved

Washington. It was the famous New York Seventh that saved the Capital. And the entire Nation, including the states in rebellion, was aware of it. Its effect on Northern mobilization was profound. Lincoln could not be absolutely sure of the response to his call for troops. The fires had to be lit and it is to the lasting credit of the Regiment that it provided one of the main sparks. The Seventh has received its orders to march! Its prominent young members are dropping everything to hasten to Washington! The Seventh has left New York! And each day the story is carried in every newspaper of the country. Every move they make is carefully chronicled. Once again they are the model civilian military organization to be copied by others. From the public relations point of view the Government was served well by the New York Seventh. The response of the North to the President's call to arms was overwhelming, but it was even more so because of this regiment.

In one other area the Seventh Regiment made an even more important contribution to the cause of the Union. As a peacetime military organization with the highest possible standards, the Seventh was a natural training school for officers. The United States historically fought its wars with volunteers. In any mobilization there was immediate and urgent need for good commissioned officers. And the value of a well-trained militia regiment in supplying this need proved itself in the Civil War. It was no wonder that McDowell's eyes lighted up when he saw the Seventh and told Captain Clark, "You have a company of officers." Nor was it to be wondered at that General Daniel E. Sickles referred to the Seventh Regiment as the "West Point of the National Guard." During the war 660 members of the Seventh served in the armed forces of the United States. Of these, 606 became commissioned officers. Among the members mustered into service in Washington in April, 1861, 345 within a few months had left the Regiment and accepted commissions in other units. The record is outstanding and establishes beyond any doubt the value of a good national guard unit.

Theodore Winthrop, in closing his chronicle of the Seventh sums up his feelings in these words:

> Character always tells. The Seventh, by good, hard, faithful work at drill, had established its fame as the most thorough militia regiment in existence. Its military and moral character were excellent. The mere name of the regiment carried weight. It took the field as if the field were a ball-room. There were myriads eager to march; but they had not made ready beforehand. Yes, the Seventh had its important share in the rescue.[4]

Epilogue
1861-1961

by Lt. Col. John F. Carroll
(formerly, Private in Company B)

The mustering out of the Seventh Regiment on June 3, 1861, was the signal for a wholesale transfer of members to the Federal forces. Their record was outstanding. Three rose to the rank of Major-General; nineteen served as Brigadier Generals; twenty-nine as colonels; forty-six as lieutenant colonels; and hundreds of others in the lower commissioned ranks. As an example of unusual service, Private Isaac Newton of Company B was chief engineer of the *Monitor* in its famous engagement with the *Merrimac*. Among those who died on the battlefield in the Civil War the name of Major Theodore Winthrop, of I Company, stands first in the Seventh Regiment's *Book of Remembrance*, which lists the heroes from each of the ten companies who lost their lives in every war. Winthrop, who fell leading a charge at Big Bethel on June 10, was the first Union volunteer killed on the field of battle.

Colonel Lefferts now set himself to the task of rebuilding the efficiency and discipline of the depleted Regiment so that "it be ready, at a moment's warning, to march at the call of the constituted authorities in defense of our flag and our country."

The next call came in May 1862 when the Union forces under McClellan were weakened by the long Peninsula campaign and Jackson's successful operations in the Shenandoah Valley. President Lincoln, fearing a Rebel move north from Richmond and an attack on the Capital, called upon Governor Morgan to send him militia to help check the enemy and defend Washington.

On May 26 at nine P.M. the Regiment embarked on the steamer *Red Jacket*, at Pier No. 2, North River, and was ferried to Elizabeth where they took a circuitous railroad trip to Baltimore via Harrisburg, Easton and Reading, arriving on May 27, at six P.M.

In the meantime, Stonewall Jackson, having accomplished his object of thwarting the junction of McDowell with McClellan, made good his retreat and Washington was out of danger. The shifting forces of the Virginia campaign, however, caused the War Department to assign the Seventh to Fort Federal Hill in order to guard the city of Baltimore. While the campaign was uneventful, the Regiment benefited by the training it received manning the heavy columbiads, howitzers, and other harbor defense weapons. Each of its companies, in addition, constantly served as prisoner-of-war escorts, conveying Confederates to various Northern prisons. On September 5, 1862, the Regiment was again mustered out of service in New York City after a period of 102 days.

On September 11, the Seventh Regiment was again called up for another tour to help bring order into a training center in east New York, where large segments of the Spinola Brigade, having used their enlistment bounty for purchase of alcohol, threatened to mutiny.

On June 17, 1863, the Regiment was again mustered into Federal service to help stem Lee's drive north into Pennsylvania which he undertook with a view to cutting off Baltimore and Washington from the North. The Seventh was assigned to guarding Forts Federal Hill and McHenry, as well as the approaches to Baltimore. However, eventually victory at Gettysburg spared Baltimore from attack.

On July 5 the Seventh Regiment was ordered to join the Third Corps at Frederick, Maryland. Here, Colonel Lefferts was appointed military governor of the city of Frederick, and temporary command of the Seventh was turned over to Lt. Col. James Price. The members of the Regiment continued to serve as prisoner-of-war escorts and highway pickets until July 14 when orders were received to return to New York to help suppress the draft riots.

This black episode of American domestic history began on Monday, July 13, when mobs burned and sacked draft offices, orphan asylums and homes of Negroes in New York City. Several hundred New Yorkers were killed or wounded before the municipal police, reinforced by the military, restored order. The Seventh Regiment remained on duty until July 21, 1863, when it was, for the third and last time during the Civil War, formally mustered out of the United States service, although it was retained on duty in New York City until September 10.

On August 18, 1863, Colonel Lefferts was appointed Brigadier-General of a New York Infantry Brigade. Because of ill health, however, he resigned from the Regiment. On June 21, 1864, Captain Emmons Clark, who was Commanding Officer of Company B and who had participated in the three Civil War campaigns of the Regiment, was elected Colonel.

On June 22, 1874, the Regiment participated in the unveiling of the Seventh Regiment Civil War Statue in Central Park at Sixty-ninth Street near Eighth Avenue. This statue, projected in 1866 in honor of those members who were killed in action or died of disease during the Civil War, is a bronze figure of heroic proportion showing a Seventh Regiment soldier on outpost duty. Executed by the American sculptor John Quincy Adams Ward, the statue itself, its granite base, and the bronze shields of the Regiment was erected at a cost of over $40,000.

The field duty during the Civil War brought home the realization that the Tompkins Market Armory was inadequate for the proper military and field training of a regiment now numbering one thousand men. Efforts were made to persuade State and City officials to secure an armory at public expense, but to no avail. Finally, in 1876 the Board of Officers opened a mail campaign to raise funds from the active and veteran members of the Regiment, friends, and business concerns of the city. Property was obtained and, on October 13, 1877, the cornerstone of the present armory building was laid at Sixty-sixth Street and Park Avenue. The actual occupation by the Regiment took place on April 26, 1880. The Armory then, as now, covered the entire block bounded by Sixty-sixth and Sixty-seventh Streets and Park and Lexington Avenues. Thus the Seventh Regiment again made military history by means of the initiative and boldness whereby they collected over $600,000 to build one of the most functional, yet attractive and unique armories in the United States, if not in the world. It is owned by the Board of Officers and the members of the Regiment. Inspired and planned by Emmons Clark, Colonel of the Seventh Regiment from 1864 to 1889, it still stands as a tribute to this former Captain of Company B.

In 1878 the Ninth Company under command of Captain William Casey spent ten days in an experimental camp at Tarrytown, New York. This camp was the forerunner of the state camp for training militia during the summer and was located at a site near Peekskill on the Hudson. Founded in 1882, the camp, presently known as Camp Smith and a prototype of the thirty-thousand-man Fort Drum, was the model for National Guard and mobilization-training camps across the country.

On April 10, 1898, nine days prior to the breaking off of diplomatic relations with Spain, Colonel Daniel Appleton and a delegation of officers from the Seventh Regiment, feeling that war was imminent, went to Washington where they were received by President William McKinley, Secretary of War Alger, and General Nelson A. Miles, Commander of the Army. They placed the Regiment at the President's disposal for any service that might be required. However, for some unknown reason, on April 20, 1898, Colonel Appleton received from Albany General Order Number Two, which directed him to assemble the Regiment and ascertain how many of its members wished to enlist as individuals. By orders of Adjutant General Tillinghast of the New York National Guard, only members of the active Regiment were to be invited to this orientation meeting. The press was positively excluded. A poll of the members revealed that they would be willing to go as a regiment but were reluctant to be called up as individuals. Even this decision was not permitted to be made public, and the absolute silence from the Regiment on Park Avenue and Sixty-sixth Street led to unfavorable newspaper conjecture, despite the fact that over two hundred individual members served as officers in the War with Spain.

Speaking after the cessation of hostilities, Senator Chauncey M. Depew reported that the Seventh Regiment had been selected to participate with the twenty-five thousand volunteers in the assault on Havana. He also stated that those matters of official history, kept secret to the detriment of the Regiment, should now be given to the public as part of the record of the war with Spain. He concluded his address by declaring that "Governor Black and General Tillinghast will long be forgotten while the Seventh Regiment will continue to live with a future of brilliant deeds that will add more to the glorious record of this distin-

guished Regiment." The following editoral appeared in
The New York Times on April 16, 1903:

We publish elsewhere in these columns a chapter of
hitherto undisclosed history which completely frees the
Seventh Regiment, N.G.N.Y., from the calumny and in-
justice to which it was subjected during and after the
Spanish War. These official documents absolutely refute
the charge that the Seventh refused to volunteer for
service wherever required, and show that it was honored by
the Secretary of War with an invitation to become part
of a column of 25,00 volunteers for a projected assault upon
Havana—an invitation that was eagerly, unconditionally
accepted by the unanimous vote of its officers. The patriotic
spirit and attitude of the Regiment during that whole
period were thoroughly understood by President McKinley,
by Secretary Alger, by Lieutenant General Miles and by
General Guy V. Henry, General Fitzhugh Lee and other
corps and division commanders. But when the first inquiry
was made as to the willingness of the Regiment to volunteer, its officers were enjoined to "perfect silence" on the
subject, and that obligation has been sacredly observed
through five long years of misrepresentation and slander.
Throughout the whole period of cruel wrong the officers
and men of the Seventh, conscious of their loyalty and
rectitude, have maintained an attitude of soldierly dignity
and self respect which is worthy of the highest praise. In
the light of the truth as officially disclosed after a review
on the evening of April 15, the Seventh stands vindicated
before the world, its purpose and motive fully justified to
the nation and its honor resplendent as the noon-day sun.
To Colonel Appleton, the gallant commander of the
Seventh and to the officers and men of that regiment, we
extend our heartiest congratulations upon this happy de-
liverance from a position of painful embarrassment in
which they were placed through no fault of their own.

The turn of the century found the Regiment in excellent numerical strength and financial condition, and the usual Armory drills were interspersed with summer encampments and rifle matches with the Queens Westminster Rifles of England.

On April 19, 1911, the observance of the Fiftieth Anniversary of the march to Washington, the full Regiment paraded up Broadway from the Old Tompkins Square armory off Lafayette Place to the reviewing stand at the St. Regis Hotel, Fifth Avenue and Fifty-fifth Street. Present were General Jacob M. Dickman, Secretary of War, representing President William H. Taft; the Governor of the State; the Mayor of New York; Major-General Leonard Wood; Major-General Frederick D. Grant; Major-General Charles F. Roe, commanding the National Guard of New York; together with a large gathering of Army, Navy, and National Guard personnel, distinguished citizens, and the remaining men of "61" who went off in response to President Lincoln's call.

The next important event was held on June 27, 1916, when at 8:30 A.M. the Regiment under the command of Colonel Willard C. Fisk, left for the Mexican border campaign. For the next five months the regiment of citizen-soldiers endured heat, insects, dust, sand, torrential rain, field problems and manuevers, north and south of the Rio Grande, little realizing how within a few months this hardship and training would be to their advantage. Three men died during this Mexican border service, but to the credit of the Seventh Regiment be it known that of the 1106 men on the roster as of June 19, 1916, the Regiment marched out 100 per cent, except one man who was in South America on business. The Regiment returned to New York on November 28, 1916, and was again mustered out of Federal service on December 2. Colonel Fisk made a special point to thank the Veterans of the Seventh for their financial support: ". . . although our motor vehicles were performing Government work, the Government was unable to furnish gasoline and oil for their use—and except for the money supplied through you, it would have been impossible to use the motor trucks which we had with us."

After a well-earned furlough, regular armory routine, tame after the Texas adventure, was resumed in January 1917. The excitement of the approaching war brought about an increase in drill attendance. On April 6, 1917, war was declared on Germany, and speculation mounted as to the role of the National Guard. Would the Seventh be called up as a unit, or would there be a repetition of the Tillinghast incident in 1898? On July 16, 1917, President Woodrow Wilson called the Seventh Regiment into the service of the United States.

The War Department at this time decided to form a division for immediate service in France, which would represent the entire United States. It was to be called the Rainbow Division, or the Forty-Second Division. Under these plans New York State was to contribute an infantry regiment. The Seventh was hopeful that it would be chosen, but, to their dismay, the Sixty-Ninth Regiment was given the assignment. To make matters worse, the War Department, in order to fill up the Sixty-Ninth, which was far under strength, ruled that every fifth Seventh Regiment enlisted man would be transferred into the Sixty-Ninth as a private, regardless of length of service or non-commissioned rank. Thus 350 members of the Seventh Regiment were shifted to the Sixty-Ninth.

The Seventh's turn was to come, however. On September 11, 1917, the Regiment marched out of the Sixty-Sixth Street Armory, down Fifth Avenue to the Twenty-Third Street Ferry, where it embarked for the troop train which was to take them to Camp Wadsworth in Spartansburg, South Carolina for training. On that day they totaled a significant number: 1917 officers and men. A new designation awaited them, however. On October 1, 1917, the historic Seventh Regiment became the One-Hundred-Seventh Infantry Regiment of New York's Twenty-Seventh Division, which fortunately was commanded by Major General John F. O'Ryan, formerly a private in Company G.

When the advance party of the One-Hundred-Seventh boarded the USS *Susquehanna* on May 9 at Newport News, Virginia, the Regiment totalled 3700 men. Entering into combat on August 10, 1918, the Seventh advanced until it helped break the Hindenburg Line. Before the armistice was signed, this "Silk Stocking Regiment" had sustained a total of 580 officers and men killed, and 1487 wounded or gassed, in action. The first member of the One-Hundred-Seventh Infantry to be killed in action was Corporal William A. Leonard of Company I, a newspaper man from Flushing, Long Island. Detailed as an observer with a British unit, he was killed on July 14, 1918. Another former member of the Seventh who was killed while serving as a sergeant with the Sixty-Ninth was the American poet Alfred Joyce Kilmer. By the time the Regiment returned to New York some two-thousand of its members had been commissioned as officers in various units of the AEF.

The spirit of the old Seventh was kept alive at the Armory during World War I by the overage or disabled veterans who largely composed the depot regiment. In the early 1920's a merger of this unit with combat-tested members of the One-Hundred-Seventh gave rise to a new organization which carried the regimental tradition through the periods of disarmament, peace movement, and depression until the outbreak of World War II. On January 6, 1922, the Regiment was entirely federalized and, under the new National

Guard designation, became known as the One-Hundred-
Seventh Infantry, NYNG, commanded by Colonel Wade
Hampton Hayes.

The lessons learned by the Allies in the early days of
World War II prompted the War Department to change
the status of the One-Hundred-Seventh Infantry to the
Two-Hundred-Seventh Coast Artillery Anti-Aircraft (Mo-
bile) on August 1, 1940. Then, months prior to Pearl
Harbor, on February 19, 1941, the Two-Hundred-Seventh
again left New York under command of Colonel Ralph C.
Tobin, this time for Camp Stewart, Georgia. Immediately
after the attack on Pearl Harbor, Battery A was detached
and sent to the Pacific Coast. In succession the Regiment
was separated into the Two-Hundred-Seventh AA group,
the Seventh, Two-Hundred-Forty-Seventh and Seven-Hun-
dred-Seventy-First AAA battalions, each one managing to
retain in its designation the magic "Seven."

At one time, elements of the Two-Hundred-Seventh were
operating in five different areas from Normandy to the
South Pacific Islands. Once more the Seventh proved its
worth as a training school for officers. In World War II
more than 2500 former members of the Regiment served as
commissioned officers in one or other branch of the armed
forces. Again, as in past mobilizations, the continuity of
the tradition of the old Seventh was maintained at the
Armory by a caretaking unit, known as the Seventh Regiment, New York State Guard.

After the cessation of global hostilities, Colonel Harry
Disston, a former member of Company L, was entrusted
with the task of rebuilding and federalizing the new One-
Hundred-Seventh Infantry NYNG. The nucleus of the new
regiment was composed of former men of the Seventh who
had served as commissioned officers in World War II. The
enlisted men were recruited from among former G.I.'s,

students of schools and colleges, and the ranks of young businessmen in New York. As the recruits brought its strength up to nearly 1300 members, the Regiment soon became the principal unit of the One-Hundred-Seventh Regimental Combat Team. Most of the old customs and traditions were retained, but to the regret of most of the Seventh, the gray uniform had to be dropped.

From the start of the Korean War, June 25, 1950, through the present protracted armistice, hundreds of former officers and men of the Seventh have served the Nation's Armed Forces in this country and overseas although no requisition was made for the Regiment as a unit, probably because, due to Selective Service quotas, only eight National Guard Divisions were called to the colors.

Upon his retirement early in 1959, Colonel Disston was promoted to Brigadier-General. He was succeeded by Colonel James M. Stewart. On March 16, 1959, General Order Number Seven from Headquarters, Division of Military and Naval Affairs, State of New York, reorganized the Regiment and designated it First Battle Group, One-Hundred-Seventh Infantry, New York Army National Guard. In contrast to a strength of twenty companies, it was reduced to seven companies. Five of these are line or rifle companies, one a headquarters company, and one a combat-support company equipped with 4.2 mortars and tanks. Thus, in sharp contrast to the old days when the Seventh Regiment stood out as the Nation's leading citizen-soldier military organization and reported directly to Presidents and Governors, it was stripped of its distinctive individuality and was subordinated as one of the five battle groups in a division.

In April 1961 the Regiment celebrated the hundredth anniversary of the march to Washington. In the presence of a handful of veterans of the Seventh and the ghosts of Colonel Lefferts and his thousand volunteers, the present colonel of the Regiment laid a wreath at the Civil War Monument in Central Park, assisted a pretty member of the Women's Army Corps in changing a sign reading "Times Square" to one reading "Seventh Regiment Square," listened while a curate of Trinity Church read from the same Book of Common Prayer that Chaplain Weston carried through the Civil War campaigns, and stood at attention while Acting-Mayor Stark pinned a long-delayed streamer on the Regimental Colors. The centennial observance was highlighted by the glowing tributes received from President of the United States John F. Kennedy, Governor Nelson Rockefeller, and Secretary of the Army Elvis Stahr. (See Appendix IV.)

The achievement of the Seventh in 1861 still serves as an illustration of the value of the citizen-soldier in time of emergency, even in an age of "pushbutton" warfare, when local military organizations are rapidly becoming absorbed into the massive structure of America's military colossus. Even though his proficiency as a soldier may not be as great as that of the full-time career Regular, the National Guardsman provides the potential for coping with local emergencies, which are best met by individuals who are familiar with their community's problems, yet who are not committed to full-time service in a standing army.

In tribute to Colonel Marshall Lefferts and a thousand New York businessmen—men who, in response to a request of the President of the United States and verbal orders of the Governor of New York State, left their businesses, their homes and their families, without questioning whether they would be paid, protected or given credit, to march to the defense of the Capital, even hiring their own transportation to arrive at their objective—these paragraphs are hopefully offered.

Notes

NOTES TO CHAPTER ONE

1. Frank Moore, *The Rebellion Record* (New York, 1867), vol. 1, p. 25.
2. J. G. Nicolay and John Hay, *Abraham Lincoln; a History* (New York, 1890), vol. 4, p. 65.
3. *Ibid.*, vol. 4, p. 258.
4. David C. Mearns, *The Lincoln Papers* (New York, 1948), vol. 2, p. 548-49.
5. Nicolay and Hay, *op. cit.*, vol. 4, p. 67.
6. *Ibid.*, p. 77-78.
7. *War of the Rebellion; a Compilation of the Official Records* (Washington, 1902), Ser. III. vol. 1, p. 67-68. Hereafter cited: W.R.
8. W.R., Ser. III, vol. 1, p. 68.
9. This correspondence is to be found complete in W.R., Ser. III, vol. 1.
10. G. T. Strong, *Diary* (New York, 1952), vol. 3, p. 109.
11. This and the preceding quotations are from Strong's diary entries, April 9-20, 1861.

NOTES TO CHAPTER TWO

1. Emmons B. Clark, *History of the Seventh Regiment of New York, 1806-1889* (New York, 1890), vol. 1, p. 106.
2. In 1835 the fourth quarter was altered by the substitution of two cannons crossed, with a blazing bomb.
3. Clark, *op. cit.*, vol. 1, p. 438-39.

4. *Ibid.*, vol. 1, p. 457.
5. *Ibid.*, vol. 1, p. 437.

NOTES TO CHAPTER THREE

1. George Templeton Strong, *Diary* (New York, 1952), vol. 3, p. 87-88.
2. Frank Moore, *The Rebellion Record* (New York, 1867), vol. 1, Docs. p. 20.
3. Emmons Clark, *History of the Seventh Regiment of New York* (New York, 1890), vol. 1, p. 468.
4. W.R., Ser. III, vol. 1, p. 40.
5. *Ibid.*, Ser. III, vol. 1, p. 41.
6. Clark, *op. cit.*, vol. 1, p. 469.
7. New York (State). *Messages from the Governors* (Albany, 1909), vol. 5, p. 357.
8. Clark, *op. cit.*, vol. 1, p. 470.
9. Frederick Phisterer, *New York in the War of the Rebellion*, 3d ed. (Albany, 1912), vol. 1, p. 14.
10. Edwin D. Morgan Papers (MS in N.Y. State Library), Correspondence: C. Gates to Morgan, April 28, 1861. Hereafter cited: Morgan Papers.
11. New York (State). *Messages from the Governors*, vol. 5, p. 400.
12. Morgan Papers (MS in N.Y. State Library), Box 42, Folder 1. State officers. Minutes of meetings, April 22, 1861.
13. William Swinton, *History of the Seventh Regiment, National Guard* (New York, 1870), p. 22.
14. Clark, *op. cit.*, vol. 1, p. 470.
15. Swinton, *op. cit.*, p. 26.
16. W.R., Ser. I, vol. 51, p. 327.
17. Clark, *op. cit.*, vol. 1, p. 470.
18. Swinton, *op. cit.*, p. 27-28.
19. Morgan Papers (MS in N.Y. State Library), Correspondence: C. W. Sandford to Morgan, April 19, 1861.
20. Swinton, *op. cit.*, p. 28. Clark's version differs in slight detail.
21. Moore, *op. cit.*, vol. 1, Docs. p. 80.
22. *Ibid.*, vol. 1, Docs. p. 148-49.
23. Swinton, *op. cit.*, p. 34-35.
24. *Ibid.*, p. 35-36.
25. Theodore Winthrop, "Our March to Washington," *Atlantic Monthly*, June, 1861, p. 745.

NOTES TO CHAPTER FOUR

1. Frank Moore, *The Rebellion Record* (New York, 1867), vol. 1, Docs. p. 149.
2. Theodore Winthrop, "Our March to Washington," *Atlantic Monthly*, June, 1861, p. 745.
3. J. Thomas Scharf and Thompson Westcott, *History of Philadelphia* (Philadelphia, 1884), vol. 1, p. 759.
4. William Swinton, *History of the Seventh Regiment, National Guard* (New York, 1870), p. 495.
5. W.R., Ser. I, vol. 2, p. 578.
6. *Ibid.*
7. Thomas W. Higginson, *Massachusetts in the Army and Navy during the War of 1861-65* (Boston, 1896), vol. 1, p. 22.
8. Benjamin F. Butler, *Butler's Book* (Boston, 1892), p. 181.
9. *Ibid.*, p. 181-84.
10. Swinton, *op. cit.*, p. 52.
11. W.R., Ser. I, vol. 2, p. 582.
12. Emmons Clark, *History of the Second Company of the Seventh Regiment* (New York, 1890), vol. 1, p. 295.
13. Emmons Clark, *History of the Seventh Regiment of New York* (New York, 1890), vol. 1, p. 478.
14. The following excerpt from *Stormy Ben Butler* by Robert S. Holzman, Ph.D., published by the Macmillan Company in 1954, may serve to throw additional light on the apparent indifference manifested by Colonel Marshall Lefferts and the other officers of the Seventh Regiment towards Brig. Gen. Benjamin F. Butler of the Massachusetts Militia whenever he attempted to exercise his command functions over them. As one interested in communications throughout New England, (a fact which was demonstrated by Lefferts' subsequent appointment as president of the New York–New England Telegraph Company), Lefferts undoubtedly had all the background necessary to form a pretty clear picture of General Benjamin F. Butler. The following is quoted from page twenty-seven of the book *Stormy Ben Butler:*

"He (Butler) had known Simon Cameron when they were both Democrats; now he wired to this leader of the Pennsylvania Republicans; 'You have called for a brigade of Massachusetts troops; why not call for a brig-

adier-general and staff? I have some hope of being detailed.' That night the desired requisition came through.
Butler's strategy had been simple; if the troops had been
ordered by the regiment, each unit would be commanded by a colonel; but a brigade obviously would
require a brigadier-general to be commander. Of course,
there were several seniors to be by-passed, but details
did not worry Butler. Early on the morning of April
16, Butler went to see James G. Carney, president of
the Bank of Mutual Redemption of Boston. Butler
realized what had occurred to no one else in those hectic
hours: it would take money to get the Massachusetts
troops to Washington. And the state had no ready
funds at hand. He spoke to the banker with great per-
suasiveness; after all, Butler's mills were good customers.
It was quickly arranged that the bank would advance
the state the necessary funds for transporting the troops,
without awaiting the necessary legislation; furthermore,
the bank would put a condition in its patriotic offer that
Butler should command the contingent. No Butler, no
loan; it was that easy. Butler then went to see the governor to ask for the command of the troops. Andrew
pointed out that there were two other generals greatly
senior to Butler; one of them, Edward Pierce, was a
veteran political ally of the governor. Pierce, in fact,
was pacing in the anteroom at that moment. At that
propitious juncture the treasurer of the Commonwealth,
Henry K. Oliver, burst into the governor's room to an-
nounce that he had just discovered there were no funds
available for transportation; the troop movement would
have to await action from the legislature. 'Governor,'
exclaimed Butler happily, 'I am aware of this condition
of things, and I can remedy it.' He said that the banks
might be persuaded to honor the state's drafts, if the
matter were approached properly. For instance, Presi-

dent Carney . . . 'Here is his letter.' The governor
got the idea immediately, but he did not have the lux-
ury of an option. Butler was given the assignment,
and Andrew had the job of making explanations to
Pierce. Pierce need not have felt that this was a slap at
his military prestige, for Butler himself announced that
he had gotten this designation because he had caused
the Boston banks to bring pressure on Andrew."

15. Swinton, *op. cit.*, p. 54.
16. New York (State), *Annual Report of the Adjutant-General,*
    1868 (Albany, 1868), p. 55.
17. W.R., Ser. I, vol. 2, p. 583.
18. *Ibid.*, p. 585.
19. Winthrop, *loc. cit.*, p. 746.
20. Moore, *op. cit.*, vol. 1, Docs. p. 150.
21. Swinton, *op. cit.*, p. 62.
22. *Ibid.*, p. 63.
23. Moore, *op. cit.*, vol. 1, p. 150.
24. *Ibid.*, vol. 1, p. 150-151.
25. Clark, *op. cit.*, vol. 1, p. 481.
26. Swinton, *op. cit.*, p. 66.

NOTES TO CHAPTER FIVE

1. Emmons Clark, *History of the Seventh Regiment of New*
   York (New York, 1890), vol. 1, p. 482-83.
2. Theodore Winthrop, "Our March to Washington," *Atlantic*
   Monthly, June, 1861, p. 748.
3. William Swinton, *History of the Seventh Regiment, National*
   Guard (New York, 1870), p. 68-69.
4. *Ibid.*, p. 69.
5. New York (State). *Annual Report of the Adjutant-General,*
   1868 (Albany, 1868), p. 56; Swinton, *op. cit.*, p. 70.
6. Swinton, *op. cit.*, p. 86. Captain Hamilton is evidently Schuyler
   Hamilton, who, however, was only a private in the Seventh
   at that time.
7. Benjamin F. Butler, *Butler's Book* (Boston, 1892), p. 198.
8. Swinton, *op. cit.*, p. 72.
9. Butler, *op. cit.*, p. 197.
10. W.R., Ser. I, vol. 2, p. 591.

11. Swinton, *op. cit.*, p. 87.
12. *Ibid.*, p. 88.
13. Clark, *op. cit.*, vol. 1, p. 484.
14. Swinton, *op. cit.*, p. 79.
15. Butler, *op. cit.*, p. 199.
16. *Ibid.*
17. Clark, *op. cit.*, vol. 1, p. 485-86.
18. Swinton, *op. cit.*, p. 90.
19. Butler, *op. cit.*, p. 199.
20. W.R., Ser. I, vol. 51, Pt. 1, p. 1274.
21. Butler, *op. cit.*, p. 201.
22. Clark, *op. cit.*, vol. 1, p. 488.
23. Butler, *op. cit.*, p. 201-202.
24. W.R., Ser. I, vol. 51, Pt. 1, p. 1272.
25. Winthrop, *loc. cit.*, p. 751.
26. Clark, *op. cit.*, vol. 1, p. 487.
27. *Ibid.*, vol. 1, p. 489-90.
28. W.R., Ser. I, vol. 2, p. 591.
29. Morgan Papers (MS in N.Y. State Library), Marshall Lefferts to Gov. Edwin D. Morgan, April 23, 1861. No other mention could be found of a courier arriving from Washington on the twenty-second, as stated by Lefferts.

NOTES TO CHAPTER SIX

1. Emmons Clark, *History of the Seventh Regiment of New York* (New York, 1890), vol. 1, p. 491.
2. Frank Moore, *The Rebellion Record* (New York, 1867), vol. 1, Docs. p. 152.
3. William Swinton, *History of the Seventh Regiment, National Guard* (New York, 1870), p. 98.
4. *Ibid.*
5. Benjamin F. Butler, *Butler's Book* (Boston, 1892), p. 203.
6. Clark, *op. cit.*, vol. 1, p. 494.
7. Theodore Winthrop, "Our March to Washington," *Atlantic Monthly*, June, 1861, p. 753-63.
8. *Ibid.*, p. 754.
9. Swinton, *op. cit.*, p. 105-106.
10. Moore, *op. cit.*, p. 153.
11. Winthrop, *loc. cit.*, p. 754-56.
12. Clark, *op. cit.*, vol. 1, p. 496.

NOTES TO CHAPTER SEVEN

1. W.R., Ser. I, vol. 2, p. 603.
2. *Ibid.*, Ser. I, vol. 51, Pt. 1, p. 335.
3. Allan Nevins, *The War for the Union* (New York, 1959), vol. 1, p. 85.
4. William Swinton, *History of the Seventh Regiment, National Guard* (New York, 1870), p. 112-113.
5. *Ibid.*, p. 113.
6. J. G. Nicolay and John Hay, *Abraham Lincoln; a History* (New York, 1890), vol. 4, p. 156-57.
7. Emmons Clark, *History of the Seventh Regiment of New York* (New York, 1890), vol. 2, p. 4.
8. Theodore Winthrop, "Washington as a Camp," *Atlantic Monthly*, July, 1861, p. 106.
9. Clark, *op. cit.*, vol. 2, p. 7.
10. *Ibid.*
11. Winthrop, *loc. cit.*, p. 109.
12. Swinton, *op. cit.*, p. 130.
13. Clark, *op. cit.*, vol. 2, p. 8-9.
14. Swinton, *op. cit.*, p. 138-140.
15. *Ibid.*, p. 158-59.
16. *Ibid.*, p. 159.
17. *Ibid.*, p. 159-60.
18. Emmons Clark, *History of the Second Company of the Seventh Regiment* (New York, 1864), p. 315-16.

NOTES TO CHAPTER EIGHT

1. William Swinton, *History of the Seventh Regiment, National Guard* (New York, 1870), p. 161-62.
2. *Ibid.*, p. 162.
3. *Ibid.*, p. 163.
4. *Ibid.*, p. 162.
5. Theodore Winthrop, "Washington as a Camp," *Atlantic Monthly*, July, 1861, p. 111.
6. Swinton, *op. cit.*, p. 169-70.
7. Winthrop, *loc. cit.*, p. 111-113.
8. Margaret Leech, *Reveille in Washington* (New York, 1941), p. 71-75.
9. Swinton, *op. cit.*, p. 174.
10. *Ibid.*

11. *Ibid.*, p. 183.
12. *Ibid.*, p. 186.
13. Emmons Clark, *History of the Second Company of the Seventh Regiment* (New York, 1864), p. 333.

NOTES TO CHAPTER NINE

1. W. R., Ser. I, vol. 2, p. 619.
2. *Ibid.*, p. 40.
3. *Ibid.*, p. 26-27.
4. Emmons Clark, *History of the Seventh Regiment of New York* (New York, 1890), vol. 2, p. 25.
5. Theodore Winthrop, "Washington as a Camp," *Atlantic Monthly*, July, 1861, p. 114.
6. William Swinton, *History of the Seventh Regiment, National Guard* (New York, 1870), p. 196.
7. Winthrop, *loc. cit.*, p. 114-115.
8. Swinton, *op. cit.*, p. 198-99.
9. Clark, *op. cit.*, vol. 2, p. 27.
10. Swinton, *op. cit.*, p. 203-204.
11. Winthrop, *loc. cit.*, p. 116.
12. Clark, *op. cit.*, vol. 2, p. 30.
13. Swinton, *op. cit.*, p. 206.
14. *Ibid.*, p. 209.
15. *Ibid.*, p. 210.
16. Clark, *op. cit.*, vol. 2, p. 32.
17. Swinton, *op. cit.*, p. 215.
18. *Ibid.*, p. 216.
19. *Ibid.*, p. 216-17.
20. Clark, *op. cit.*, vol. 2, p. 37.
21. *Ibid.*, vol. 2, p. 37-38.
22. *Ibid.*, vol. 2, p. 38.

NOTES TO CHAPTER TEN

1. "Theodore Winthrop," *Atlantic Monthly*, August, 1801, p. 251.
2. William Swinton, *History of the Seventh Regiment, National Guard* (New York, 1870), p. 463.
3. *Ibid.*, p. 452.
4. Theodore Winthrop, "Washington as a Camp," *Atlantic Monthly*, July, 1861, p. 118.

Appendix I
Roll of Honor

THE FOLLOWING is Col. Emmons Clark's list of those members of the Seventh Regiment who saw service during the Civil War. It is probably incomplete and may contain a few inaccuracies. It is nevertheless the most extensive list available.

First Company.

Capt. C. Graham Bacon.
Capt. Robert Bailey.
Capt. Augustus Belknap, Jr.
Lieut. Charles Belknap.
Priv. L. H. Broome.
Lieut. Charles W. Chauncey.
Capt. W. H. Cooper.
Capt. George F. Cooke.
Maj. W. H. Corsa.
Sergt. George W. Cowen.
Surg. J. C. Dalton.
Capt. B. F. Davis.
Col. W. J. Denslow.
Lieut.-Col. A. D'Orville.

Capt. H. C. Ellis.
Lieut. Robert D. Evans.
Capt. James Fairgrieve.
Sergt. George W. Freeland.
Lieut.-Col. O. H. Hart.
Capt. Henry I. Hayden.
Capt. C. E. Huberer.
Lieut. T. S. Kirkland.
Capt. George B. Le Fort.
Capt. Charles H. Lyon.
Maj. Frederick Mears.
Lieut.-Col. F. E. McIlvaine.
Capt. A. B. McGowan.
Sergt. J. Morrow.

Lieut. W. A. Nichols.
Lieut. R. H. Plass.
Paymr. William V. Porter.
Lieut. C. L. Reynolds.
Capt. George W. Ring.
Capt. Theodore Russell.
Lieut. John W. Sibell.
Maj. F. D. Slocomb.
Lieut. Beneke C. Stout.
Lieut.-Col. Charles N. Swift.

Lieut. Charles J. Theriott.
Lieut. E. C. Tiffany.
Lieut. Charles S. Tripler.
Surg. Eustace Trenor.
Surg. John Trenor.
Capt. J. J. Trenor.
Lieut. S. C. Thwaite.
Capt. A. B. Villeplaite.
Lieut. M. W. Whitlock.
Lieut. W. P. Wheeler.

Second Company.

Capt. Henry H. Alden.
Col. William H. Allen.
Capt. Richard Allison.
Maj. Charles Appleby.
Sergt. Evert S. Bedford.
Capt. Edward Bernard.
Lieut.-Col. George A. Bernard.
Capt. J. F. Bisbee.
Capt. Richard R. Brouner.
Gen. William H. Browne.
Capt. John C. Bloomfield.
Lieut. A. Martin Burtis.
Lieut.-Col. William Chalmers.
Lieut. William O. Chapman.
Maj. Joseph J. Comstock.
Maj. James C. Cooley.
Lieut.-Col. Robert Cottier.
Gen. Abram Duryee.
Lieut.-Col. Alexander Douglas.
Paymr. William L. Darling.
Capt. James J. De Barry.
Lieut. Lewis G. Dudley.
Capt. Jacob Duryee.
Lieut. Henry B. Dyer.

Capt. William Edwards.
Capt. Charles Emerson.
Col. Noah L. Farnham.
Lieut. Benjamin Gregory.
Paymr. Henry S. Gregory.
Paymr. Oscar Hall.
Lieut. Norwood A. Halsey.
Engr. R. F. Hatfield.
Capt. Townsend L. Hatfield.
Lieut.-Col. Henry G. Healy.
Capt. Henry H. Harrall.
Maj. William W. Harrall.
Purser Thomas W. K. Holder.
Gen. Edward Jardine.
Capt. Eugene Kelty.
Maj. James S. King.
Maj. John Lawrence.
Maj. Robert W. Leonard.
Gen. J. Henry Liebenau.
Master J. Walter Mackie.
Lieut.-Col. David W. Marshall.
Lieut.-Col. Joseph E.
    McFarland.
Corp. Frederick A. McKay.

Capt. James A. McMickin.
Capt. David Miller.
Lieut. James Miller.
Lieut. Silas A. Miller.
Lieut.-Col. David I. Miln.
Lieut.-Col. James B. Mix.
Gen. Edward L. Molineux.
Engr. Isaac Newton.
Col. Theodore W. Parmelee.
Capt. W. D. Pearne.
Capt. Moses L. M. Peixotto.
Sergt. Gurdon S. Phipps.
Lieut.-Col. Henry M. Porter.
Lieut. De Van Postley.
Lieut.-Col. James W. Powell.
Lieut. Glenn Putnam.
Lieut. Charles R. Reed.
Paymr. W. V. N. Rosedale.

Lieut.-Col. Henry F. Savage.
Gen. Alexander Shaler.
Capt. Simon W. Scott.
Capt. George W. Selover.
Col. George W. Stillwell.
Capt. Charles H. Sterling.
Lieut. Eliphalet W. Stratton.
Lieut.-Col. Charles H. Tay.
Capt. Lucien M. Thayer.
Lieut. Henry J. Tiemann.
Capt. George F. E. Tybring.
Capt. Charles S. Van Norden.
Lieut. A. H. Vroom.
Capt. Almar P. Webster.
Capt. E. B. Webster.
Capt. G. V. Weir.
Capt. William H. Williams.
Capt. James Wood.

Third Company.

Capt. George W. Bacon.
Col. William P. Baily.
Lieut. John H. Baker.
Capt. Eugene F. Benedict.
Lieut.-Col. George N.
  Bomford.
Lieut.-Col. John L. Brower.
Lieut. Charles L. Brown.
Capt. W. C. Burton.
Lieut. George B. Butler, Jr.
Capt. A. S. Bush.
Lieut.-Col. W. H.
  Cheesbrough.
Col. Clinton G. Colgate.
Paymr. L. P. Crane.
Lieut. Gardner K. Doughty.

Lieut.-Col. Thomas Elliot.
Capt. Latham A. Fish.
Adjt. Philip D. Gulager.
Capt. Moses C. Hagadorn.
Gen. Joseph E. Hamblin.
Lieut.-Col. Robert McD. Hart.
Priv. B. F. Hillery.
Capt. William Howland.
Capt. Frederick Hurst.
Maj. Frank Jeffrey.
Maj. Edgar Ketchum.
Lieut. Lewis M. Johnson.
Capt. John W. Lewis, Jr.
Sergt. David O. Logan.
Capt. Henry W. T. Mali.
Paymr. J. W. Mangam.

Lieut. Charles M. Marsh.
Gen. Gilbert H. McKibben.
Capt. Samuel G. Milligan.
Capt. Henry H. Mott.
Lieut. George H. Packwood.
Lieut. William H. Peck.
Lieut. Ambrose H. Purdy.
Capt. Herman G. Radcliffe.
Sergt. Louis L. Robbins.
Lieut. Alexander M. C. Smith, Jr.
Maj. Thomas F. Smith.
Lieut. Joseph M. Stamford.
Capt. Waldo Sprague.
Capt. Theodore Stagg.
Sergt. Hugh B. Thomson.
Gen. Henry E. Tremain.

Lieut. Walter R. Tremain.
Capt. William W. Tracy.
Lieut.-Col. Thomas R. Turnbull.
Capt. George Tuthill.
Surg. Thomas B. Tuthill.
Sergt. Lewis C. Updike.
U. S. N. James B. Van Cleef.
Lieut. William A. Verplanck.
Adjt. William S. Watkins.
Capt. George H. Wheaton.
Surg. James M. Wilson.
Maj. Albert H. Winslow.
Priv. Charles F. Wisewell.
Maj. David F. Wright.
Gen. John G. Wright.
Col. William E. Van Wyck.

Fourth Company.

Lieut.-Col. Edwin S. Babcock.
Gen. William B. Barton.
Lieut. Henry C. Belden.
Capt. Edward Benson.
Lieut. Albert C. Bendick.
Lieut. Joseph Cantrell.
Col. Alford B. Chapman.
Ensign Walter Cooper.
Adjt. E. Benson Cox.
Capt. George A. Crocker.
Lieut.-Col. William H. Crocker.
Lieut. William E. Fiske.
Lieut. Henry J. Foster.
Lieut. S. F. B. Gillespie.
Sergt. Louis N. Gulager.
Gen. William Gurney.
Capt. Edward A. Harrison.

Lieut. Charles R. Hickox.
Adjt. Leonard Hay.
Sergt. William A. Jackson.
Sergt. John Jarvis.
Sergt. R. L. Johnson.
Lieut.-Col. Edward H. Little.
Capt. John L. Little.
Lieut. A. V. B. Lockrow.
Col. James E. Mallon.
Lieut.-Col. Alexander S. Marshall.
Lieut. A. C. Merritt.
Lieut. Aaron J. Mixsell.
Lieut. John E. Moies.
Lieut.-Col. Samuel W. McPherson.
Lieut.-Col. Charles J. Murphy.

Lieut. Joseph Neustaedter.
Priv. H. C. Nichols.
Gen. Robert Nugent.
Sergt. Edward J. Olssen.
Maj. Mortimer B. Owen.
Lieut. William H. Roome.
Lieut.-Col. George Sangster.
Capt. J. Daniel Schuller.

Maj. Frank K. Smith.
Sergt. Milton Smith.
Lieut. Samuel J. Smith.
Sergt. Archibald A. Snodgrass.
Lieut.-Col. Z. L. Spaulding.
Capt. Samuel H. Starr.
Capt. Peter B. Steel.
Lieut. Joseph B. Stevenson.

Fifth Company.

Lieut.-Col. Thomas J. Addis.
Capt. James Bell.
Corp. Samuel A. Beers.
Capt. E. D. Benedict.
Capt. A. Biddle.
Capt. George W. Bissell.
Sergt. John Bolton.
Capt. William A. Brusle, Jr.
Purser Henry C. Braisted.
Capt. C. R. Cargill.
Sergt. John B. Clapp.
Capt. William Coles.
Capt. F. H. Corrie.
Lieut. Frederick Creighton, Jr.
Sergt. A. S. Doremus.
Corp. David M. Doremus.
Lieut. Robert Eagan.
Capt. Edward S. Earle.
Maj. Francis S. Earle.
Engr. Frederick Eckel.
Sergt. Frederick E. Edgar.
Adjt. Frank C. Filley.
Gen. Louis Fitzgerald.
Sergt. Augustus Fleet.
Maj. Alfred Foote.
Adjt. Charles J. Frothingham.

Capt. F. Grain, Jr.
Lieut. Levi Grosvenor.
Maj. William P. Halsted.
Capt. J. L. Hawkins.
Lieut. C. O. F. Haynes.
Capt. G. M. Husted.
Capt. B. R. Keefler.
Lieut.-Col. J. G. Kappner.
Lieut. S. M. Kellinger.
Lieut.-Col. W. E. Kidder.
Lieut. William H. Kingsland.
Capt. George W. Lewis.
Capt. John S. Loud.
Corp. John B. McIntyre.
Lieut. Benjamin T. Martin.
Sergt. Willis McDonald.
Lieut. S. E. L. Mitchell.
Gen. J. J. Morrison.
Lieut. George W. Murray.
Gen. James R. O'Beirne.
Sergt. William J. Oliphant.
Ensign H. M. Patterson.
Lieut. W. A. Prentiss, Jr.
Sergt. George A. Price.
Capt. Peter A. Rink.
Lieut. Thomas J. Roberts.

Capt. William H. Romaine.
Capt. Francis A. Silva.
Sergt. George B. Thorne.
Maj. M. A. Stearns.
Sergt. John M. Smith.
Lieut. Noah B. Stokely.
Sergt. T. G. Thorne.
Lieut. Henry M. Timolat.

Lieut.-Col. George Tucker.
Capt. William H. Underhill.
Maj. Philo Vosburg.
Capt. F. E. Waldron.
Capt. William L. Watson
Capt. James L. Waugh.
Capt. Robert Wheaton.
Lieut. L. L. Young.

Sixth Company.

Col. Alexander Annan.
Capt. Henry Arnold.
Gen. Lewis T. Barney.
Gen. Charles G. Bartlett.
Lieut.-Col. James W.
  Benkard, Jr.
Capt. Jabez H. Bradbury.
Maj. Clarence S. Brown.
Lieut. George L. Browning.
Capt. Churchill J. Cambreling.
Capt. Samuel Carey.
Lieut.-Col. Lynde Catlin.
Capt. P. R. Chadwick.
Lieut.-Col. Floyd Clarkson.
Capt. Poinsett Cooper.
Capt. Edward A. Cowdrey.
Lieut.-Col. Frank H. Cowdrey.
Capt. Edward Cozzens.
Capt. James D. W. Cutting.
Lieut.-Col. Louis L. Cuvillier.
Capt. Archibald Douglas.
Lieut. Charles N. Dubois.
Capt. Robert S. Dumont.
Gen. Jacob E. Duryee.
Paymr. Theodore O. Ebaugh.
Capt. George Edgar.

Capt. Joseph S. Edsall.
Lieut. E. A. Edwards.
Lieut. C. H. Ellingwood.
Lieut. Asher M. Ellsworth.
Capt. Joel B. Erhardt.
Lieut. Joseph F. Evans.
Capt. H. L. Fearing.
Lieut.-Col. George W. Ford.
Lieut. James W. Ford.
Lieut. G. W. Forney.
Gen. John A. Foster.
Capt. John W. French.
Lieut. James Gordon, Jr.
Capt. S. Augustus Gould.
Capt. Charles C. Haight.
Maj. Edward L. Halsted.
Lieut.-Col. Richard F. Halsted.
Gen. Schuyler Hamilton.
Lieut. John F. Hardy.
Capt. Henry W. Hicks, Jr.
Lieut.-Col. Samuel J. Hopkins.
Capt. Stephen T. Hosmer.
Capt. Francis A. Howell.
Col. Harmon D. Hull.
Lieut. John L. Hyde.
Capt. Julian James.

Maj. Rufus King, Jr.
Capt. A. J. Lamb.
Lieut.-Col. Samuel B. Lawrence.
Gen. William H. Lawrence.
Capt. Mortimer Livingston.
Capt. Theodore Mallaby, Jr.
Maj. Edward Marrenner.
Col. Thomas B. Marsh.
Sergt. George L. Middlebrook.
Maj. Lindley M. H. Miller.
Sergt. George W. Munson.
Col. Charles L. Norton.
Capt. George H. Palmer.
Paymr. William M. Palmer.
Lieut.-Col. Tatnall Paulding.
Paymr. Charles B. Perry.
Maj. Horatio Potter, Jr.
Lieut. Robert Potter.
Capt. James P. Raymond.
Lieut. S. H. Robbins.
Lieut.-Col. William P. Roome.
Maj. Philip Schuyler, Jr.
Col. Robert G. Shaw.
Lieut. H. M. G. Shaw.
Capt. Alexander E. Sheldon.
Capt. Augustus Shimmel.
Lieut. Charles G. Smedberg.

Lieut.-Col. William R. Smedberg.
Chaplain J. Tuttle Smith.
Col. William W. Stephenson.
Lieut. Henry A. Still.
Capt. Edward C. Sturgis.
Adjt. Charles T. Sutton.
Capt. Deforest H. Thomae.
Capt. Gould H. Thorp.
Lieut. Frederic A. Tracy.
Capt. Fanning C. Tucker.
Capt. William G. Ulshoeffer.
Lieut. William H. Vance.
Lieut. Charles F. Van Duser.
Lieut. James H. Van Nostrand.
Maj. Philip L. Van Rensselaer.
Capt. George R. Vernon.
Lieut. James B. Vose.
Capt. Robert P. Warren.
Master Benjamin S. Weeks.
Lieut. Edward W. West.
Lieut. Roswell Weston.
Paymr. F. Wheeler.
Engr. George H. White.
Lieut.-Col. William Winthrop.
Surg. Wilmer S. Wood.
Lieut. George W. Young.

Seventh Company.

Capt. R. S. Alcoke.
Capt. C. A. Alvord, Jr.
Lieut.-Col. Smith W. Anderson.
Capt. T. H. Annable.
Capt. Edwin Bishop.

Lieut.-Col. George Bishop.
Capt. Edmund Blunt.
Lieut. A. Schuyler Bogart.
Gen. R. N. Bowerman.
Paymr. C. J. Breck.
Capt. A. H. Britton.

Col. Harvey S. Chatfield.
Lieut.-Col. John N. Coyne.
Lieut.-Col. Abraham Denike.
Maj. E. Donaldson.
Sergt. H. Duncan.
Capt. James Duryee.
Lieut.-Col. William B. C. Duryee.
Maj. Edward Eddy, Jr.
Lieut. John H. Gardner, Jr.
Lieut. J. Graham Gardner.
Lieut. W. F. Geisse.
Capt. Lewis B. Goodnow.
Col. E. R. Goodrich.
Gen. Charles A. Hartwell.
Capt. E. J. Henry.
Lieut. T. W. B. Hughes.
Lieut. William D. Hale.
Maj. Robert A. Hutchins.
Lieut. James H. Ingersoll.
Gen. Samuel B. Jones.
Maj. P. C. Kingsland.
Capt. Louis H. Lent.
Col. John P. Leverich.
Capt. James H. Lounsberry.
Sergt. Thomas H. Millie.
Capt. L. R. McDonough.
Capt. George A. Morey.
Maj. John D. Moriarty.

Col. Edward Murray.
Adjt. Albert A. Neal.
Col. Jacob J. Noah.
Col. William Northridge.
Capt. Fitz-James O'Brien.
Capt. John Oldershaw.
Paymr. William Patten.
Lieut. Frederick H. Pinkney.
Capt. James Plant.
Maj. Eugene F. Roberts.
Lieut. J. F. Robinson.
Gen. Allen Rutherford.
Priv. William E. Schenck.
Capt. F. J. Steers.
Lieut.-Col. George H. Stevens.
Maj. Robert K. Stewart.
Capt. R. Burnett Smith.
Lieut.-Col. Henry Street.
Priv. Thomas S. Timpson.
Gen. F. E. Trotter.
Lieut.-Col. Samuel Truesdell.
Col. Charles Turnbull.
Capt. William H. Underhill.
Maj. Henry Vander Weyde.
Adjt. E. Van Ness.
Capt. Theodore C. Vidal.
Capt. William J. Williams.
Lieut. H. J. Winters.

Eighth Company.

Capt. James T. Baker.
Paymr. John M. Baker.
Maj. Robert P. Barry.
Sergt. Charles A. Barton.
Priv. Eugene Bissell.

Capt. Clarence A. Blake.
Lieut. N. H. Baylis.
Corp. H. N. Bradstreet.
Maj. William W. Buckley.
Ensign H. D. Burdett.

Lieut.-Col. William L. M. Burger.
Lieut.-Col. Charles H. Burtis.
Paymr. Frank Cargill.
Capt. W. J. Carleton.
Maj. James S. Casey.
Maj. Oliver Cotter.
Lieut. Thomas W. Dick.
Lieut. Theodore S. Dumont.
Surg. William B. Eager, Jr.
Capt. Henry C. Ellis.
Capt. William I. Ellis.
Capt. Amos F. Eno.
Lieut. Robert O. N. Ford.
Capt. S. J. Foster.
Gen. H. S. Gansevoort.
Capt. James B. Grant.
Capt. F. H. Grant.
Adjt. William Henderson.
Gen. John Hendrickson.
Lieut. Henry W. Hubbell, Jr.
Capt. John H. Hull.
Capt. James C. Hyatt.
Paymr. T. Granville Hoyt.
Lieut. William C. Jacobson.
Lieut. E. R. Johnson.
Priv. J. Lawrence Keese.
Capt. Edward C. Kittle.
Lieut. E. Kirby.
Capt. J. N. T. Levick.

Capt. Walter Lloyd.
Capt. E. S. Mann.
Capt. William D. Mansfield.
Gen. John McNeil.
Maj. Charles E. Mears.
Capt. Albert V. Meeks.
Capt. S. A. Mellick.
Maj. E. R. Merriman.
Capt. Theodore W. Morgan.
Col. Albert P. Moulton.
Lieut.-Col. H. S. Murray.
Capt. E. B. Norton.
Gen. John H. Oley.
Paymr. William H. Owen.
Adjt. Lewis O. Parmelee.
Lieut. Frederick T. Peet.
Lieut.-Col. Charles E. Prescott.
Lieut. Edward L. Postley.
Capt. Philip C. Rogers.
Adjt. J. F. Satherwaite.
Gen. Charles E. Smith.
Lieut. Charles L. Smith.
Capt. Adrian Spear.
Lieut.-Col. Percy B. Spear.
Scrgt. William E. Sterr.
Capt. E. N. K. Talcott.
Lieut. J. J. Webber.
Capt. J. Howard Wells.
Lieut. J. D. Wickham.
Capt. George C. Williams.

Ninth Company.

Capt. J. C. Ball.
Sergt. J. Barrett.
Lieut. A. R. Barritt.
Lieut. L. W. Brainard.

Col. William S. Bramhall.
Capt. Theodore H. Bush.
Lieut.-Col. W. B. Coan.
Engr. A. M. Cummings.

Lieut. Barry Davies.
Lieut. G. D. Davis.
Lieut. George H. Dayton.
Sergt. Fordred Drayson.
Lieut. Clinton Eddy.
Capt. Franklin Ellis.
Lieut. D. R. Franklin.
Capt. Samuel Giberson.
Capt. L. O. Goodridge.
Gen. E. E. Graves.
Master J. Russell Howell.
Sergt. R. M. Harmstead.
Capt. Frank M. Kelley.
Gen. Nathaniel P. Lane.
Lieut. J. P. Manning.
Priv. James Martin.
Capt. Henry Matthews.
Lieut. R. A. Hills.
Sergt. T. A. McCrossen.
Gen. N. B. McLaughlin.
Maj. B. B. Miller.

Engr. Edward B. Mingay.
Col. R. T. Mitchell.
Lieut. G. C. Moore.
Lieut. Theodore Oliver.
Capt. John R. Paxton.
Capt. Nelson Plato.
Capt. Fenton Rockwell.
Capt. John Rodgers.
Surg. A. Orimel Shaw.
Lieut. A. B. Spier.
Capt. T. B. Stout.
Maj. Ivan Tailof.
Lieut. George F. Van Brunt.
Capt. John Walker.
Lieut. George M. Wells.
Capt. William Wheeler.
Lieut. D. W. White.
Lieut. James G. White.
Maj. William H. Wiley.
Maj. Theodore Winthrop.

Tenth Company.

Capt. Hoffman Atkinson.
Lieut. W. Henry Bradshaw.
Lieut. Milnor Brown.
Capt. Thomas B. Bunting.
Maj. John H. Coster.
Lieut. J. G. Costar.
Col. Charles R. Coster.
Lieut. Whittingham Cox.
Lieut. John L. Churchill.
Paymr. Frank Clark.
Maj. Samuel Dana.
Lieut.-Col. J. L. De Peyster.
Capt. Edward D'Hervilly.

Lieut. William Dimmock.
Lieut. David Drake.
Maj. C. J. Dubois.
Capt. Thomas Freeborn.
Adjt. Charles A. Gadsden.
Maj. Theodore K. Gibbs.
Capt. Richard H. Greene.
Lieut. Richard B. Hall.
Lieut. Herbert H. Hall.
Lieut. John G. Hecksher.
Capt. H. H. Holbrook.
Lieut.-Col. Edward P. Hollis-
ter.

Adjt. Effingham T. Hyatt.
Lieut.-Col. William A. Kobbé.
Col. F. W. Leggett.
Lieut.-Col. Francis L. Leland.
Maj. Thomas Lord, Jr.
Capt. Henry W. Miller.
Capt. George M. Miller.
Capt. Lewis Morris.
Maj. R. L. Morris.
Capt. Robert Morris.
Maj. Nathan F. Moss.
Lieut. J. Delancey Neill.
Gen. J. Frederick Pierson.
Lieut.-Col. Henry L. Pierson.
Col. Clifton K. Prentiss.
Capt. J. Henry Plume.
Adjt. Fritz Robert.
Paymr. William H. Reid.
Capt. Henry A. Sand.
Capt. Robert S. Seabury.

Maj. William H. Schiefflin.
Capt. F. A. Schermerhorn.
Lieut. David J. Scott.
Adjt. W. H. M. Sistare.
Capt. J. Stewart Slosson.
Lieut. Wright Staples.
Adjt. J. Brainerd Taylor.
Sergt. Ed. F. Thompson.
Lieut. W. W. Tompkins.
Surg. A. Van Cortlandt.
Maj. Stephen Van Rensselaer.
Capt. E. B. Van Winkle.
Gen. Egbert L. Viele.
Adjt. W. S. Wallace.
Maj. O. Wetmore, Jr.
Priv. Edward B. Welles.
Adjt. John C. White.
Lieut.-Col. John B. Winslow.
Engr. Charles Winter.

Total number of members of the Seventh Regiment, N.G., S.N.Y., who served in the Regular and Volunteer Army and Navy of the United States during the Great Rebellion:

First Company	48		Seventh Company		67
Second "	83		Eighth "		69
Third "	62		Ninth "		49
Fourth "	48		Tenth "		64
Fifth "	68				
Sixth "	104		Total		662

NAMES AND RANK OF THE MEMBERS OF THE SEV-
ENTH REGIMENT, NATIONAL GUARD, S.N.Y., WHO
WERE KILLED OR DIED OF DISEASE OR WOUNDS
IN THE UNITED STATES SERVICE, 1861-1865:

First Company.

Captain George B. Le Fort, killed at the Wilderness, Va.
Captain Theodore Russell, killed at Fair Oaks, Va.
Captain J. J. Trenor, killed at Fair Oaks, Va.

Second Company.

Captain Henry H. Alden, killed at Ball's Bluff, Va.
Colonel Noah L. Farnham, died from wounds, Bull Run, Va.
 (1861).
Captain Eugene Kelty, killed at Baton Rouge, La.
Lieutenant Silas A. Miller, killed at Gettysburg, Pa.
Sergeant Gurdon S. Phipps, killed at Bristow Station, Va.
Lieutenant D. Van Postley, killed at Donaldsonville, La.

Third Company.

Lieutenant John A. Baker, died at Fort Federal Hill, Md.
Lieutenant-Colonel Robert Mc. D. Hart, killed at Cedar Creek,
 Va.
Captain Frederick Hurst, died from wounds, Charleston, S. C.
Captain Samuel G. Mulligan, died on the Rapidan, Va.
Captain H. G. Radcliffe, killed at Murfreesboro', Tenn.
Lieutenant R. Tremaine, died at Suffolk, Va.

Fourth Company.

Colonel Alford B. Chapman, killed at the Wilderness, Va.
Captain Edward A. Harrison, killed at Bull Run, Va. (1862).
Colonel James E. Mallon, killed at Bristow Station, Va.
Lieutenant John E. Moies, died at New Orleans, La.
Captain Samuel H. Starr, died at Vicksburg, Miss.

Fifth Company.

Lieutenant-Colonel Thomas J. Addis, died from wounds.

Captain A. Biddle, died in the Shenandoah Valley, Va.

Captain George W. Bissell, died in the United States service.

Sergeant Augustus Fleet, killed at Fair Oaks, Va.

Lieutenant William H. Kingsland, died at Andersonville, Ga.

Captain George W. Lewis, died from wounds, Harrison's Landing, Va.

Lieutenant Henry M. Timolat, killed in the Shenandoah Valley, Va.

Lieutenant-Colonel George Tucker, died at New Orleans, La.

Sixth Company.

Captain Henry Arnold, killed at Olustee, Fla.

Captain Edward A. Cowdrey, mortally wounded at Five Forks, Va.

Captain Asher M. Ellsworth, died at Port Hudson, La.

Captain Henry W. Hicks, mortally wounded at Port Hudson, La.

Major Lindley M. H. Miller, died in New York, June, 1864.

Colonel Robert G. Shaw, killed at Fort Wagner, S. C.

Lieutenant Charles G. Smedberg, died in camp near Falmouth, Va.

Lieutenant Frederick A. Tracy, died at New York, June 3, 1862.

Lieutenant Charles F. Van Duser, killed at Gaines's Mills, Va.

Lieutenant James H. Van Nostrand, died a prisoner at Lynchburg, Va.

Seventh Company.

Lieutenant A. S. Bogert, died from wounds, Fair Oaks, Va.

Captain Louis H. Lent, killed at Fort Wagner, S. C.

Captain Fitz-James O'Brien, died from wounds, Blooming Gap, Va.

Captain George A. Morey, died at Harrison's Landing, Va.

Lieutenant-Colonel George H. Stevens, killed at Gettysburg, Pa.

Captain William J. Williams, killed at Fair Oaks, Va.
Private William E. Schenck, drowned in New York Harbor.

Eighth Company.

Private J. Lawrence Keese, killed at Washington, D. C.
Captain S. A. Mellick, died at Fortress Monroe, Va.
Adjutant Lewis O. Parmelee, killed at Antietam, Md.
Lieutenant Edward L. Postley, died in Red River campaign, Arkansas.

Ninth Company.

Major Theodore Winthrop, killed at Great Bethel, Va.
Captain William Wheeler, killed at Culp's Farm, Va.
Sergeant Fordred Drayson, killed at Cold Harbor, Va.

Tenth Company.

Lieutenant Milnor Brown, killed at Gettysburg, Pa.
Adjutant Charles A. Gadsden, killed at Camden, N. C.
Captain J. Henry Plume, killed at Manassas, Va.
Colonel Clifton K. Prentiss, died from wounds, Petersburg, Va.
Captain Henry A. Sand, killed at Antietam, Md.
Captain Robert S. Seabury, killed at Spottsylvania, Va.
Captain Wright Staples, killed in the Wilderness, Va.
Private Edward B. Welles, died at Baltimore, Md.

Appendix II
Poems and Songs of the Seventh

THE SEVENTH

Leaped to their feet a thousand men,
  Their voices echoing far and near;
"We go, we care not, where or when;
  Our country calls us, we are here!"

Who talks of playing soldier now?
  Who flings the dandy in their teeth?
As the blood flushes o'er each brow
  From fearless hearts that beat beneath.

Down the long street the column pours,
  With shining ranks and measured tread;
While rings along the island shores,
  A shout that might awake the dead.

From women's lips and bearded men
  A million blessings fall in showers;
"They go, they care not where or when
  God bless the Seventh, they are ours!" *

* *Harper's Weekly*, April 27, 1861, p. 259. Author unknown.

THE MARCH OF THE "SEVENTH"

What means this eager rush? whence this commotion?
Why surge the people thus, like a lashed ocean?
See, the vast multitude, crowding and craving;
See, from each lofty staff stars and stripes waving!

Banners from balcony, banners from steeple,
Banners from house to house, draping the people;
Banners upborne by all, men, women, children,
Banners on horses' fronts, flashing, bewild'ring.

Hark! there's a trumpet-blast strikes on the hearing;
Now the quick drum-beat comes rapidly nearing;
Blue forms with clubs in hand, steadily banding,
Through the compacted crowd pathway demanding.

Drums beat, and trumpets sound, louder and louder,
Bugles and cornets mix deep tones and prouder;
Whose is that solid front? whose is that thick step?
Whose, but the "Seventh's" tread, moves to that quickstep?

On comes the Regiment, like to none other;
Who has not in its ranks loved son or brother?
If he has none of these, not e'en a cousin,
He served himself in it, years by the dozen.

Know ye the city's heart in that mass mingles?
Hear, the responsive throb everywhere tingles!
Now, as they're moving past, shout, sob, and greeting,
Love's deep devotion they're constantly meeting.

See, 'midst the serried ranks, none now objecting,
Hundreds of laymen the flanks seem protecting,
Crowding between platoons, filling the spaces,
Many a manly form steadily paces!

Those are the fathers, proud eyes overflowing,
On Freedom's altar their best blood bestowing;
Gladly they give their sons, each true heart bleeding,
Offering the noblest to Liberty's needing.

Oh, 'tis a costly gift now they are bringing,
And on their country's shrine willingly flinging;
One gives five sons, others their four, three, two—
Ye who have sons there, ah, how do I envy you!

There stands brave Anderson, watching them, breathless—
Glory's new-born son, whose name now is deathless;
Look he not proudly on? Soon they espy him,
Loud rings their homage cheer, as they pass by him.

Why does he drop a tear? why is he weeping,
As that majestic march by him is sweeping?
Ah, he beholds in them, earnest and steady,
Hearts like his noble own, for sacrifice ready.

He knows the savage horde lately contending,
Not as our sires fought, Justice defending,
But, with the tiger's fangs, stealthily seeking
Power the weak to scourge, 'midst tears and shrieking.

Hero of Sumter! thy name is forever
Coupled with Glory, and ne'er will we sever
"Manhood and Anderson." Freedom's libation
Pours forth from million hearts through all the nation.

Vengeance is now the cry, no more betraying;
Treating with traitors is senseless delaying;
Sons of the Bay State their Sumner remember;
Wrongs to be righted now wake from their slumber.

Pass on the battle-cry! sound it forth, trumpter!
Hand it from man to man—"Sumner and Sumter!"
Hark! now from Baltimore comes, madly driven,
One more foul insult that can't be forgiven.

Go forth, then, gallant hearts, bearing the casket
Holding our city's blood—seek not to mask it!
Fling it before you far, fight your way to it;
Stay them not, Maryland, or you will rue it.

Fathers are arming fast, mothers are praying,
While you are noble deeds skilfully playing;
Soon we will follow you; New York is coming!
Hark, do you hear the rush, like Niagara booming?

Onward, then, "Seventh!" delay not, nor waver!
Rush to fair Freedom's side, guard her and save her!
Give the vile vulture blood-kites, buzzards, marauders—
The feast that they're lusting for from their own borders! *

R.S.O., New York *Tribune*, April 23, 1861

THE SEVENTH
by Fitz-James O'Brien
Air—"Gilla Machree."

I.

Och! we're the boys
That hearts desthroys
Wid making love and fighting;
We take a fort,
The girls we court,
But most the last delight in.
To fire a gun
Or raise some fun,
To us is no endeavor;
So let us hear
One hearty cheer—
The Seventh's lads for ever!

* Quoted in Frank Moore, "Poetry and Incidents," *The Rebellion Record* (New York, 1867), vol. I, p. 48.

CHORUS:
 For we're the boys
 That hearts desthroys
Wid making love and fighting;
 We take a fort,
 The girls we court,
But most the last delight in.

II.

 There's handsome Joe,
 Whose constant flow
Of merriment unfailing,
 Upon the tramp
 Or in the camp,
Will keep our hearts from ailing.
 And B—— and Chat
 Who might have sat
For Pythias and Damon.
 Och! whin they get
 Their heavy wet,
They get as high as Haman.

CHORUS:
 For we're the boys . . .

III.

 Like Jove above
 We're fond of love
But fonder still of victuals;
 Wid turtle steaks
 An' codfish cakes
We always fills our kittles.
 To dhrown aich dish,
 We dhrinks like fish,
And Mumm's the word we utther;

An' thin we swill
Our Leoville,
That oils our throats like butther.

CHORUS:
For we're the boys . . .

IV.

We make from hay
A splindid tay,
From beans a gorgeous coffee;
Our crame is prime
Wid chalk and lime—
In fact, 'tis quite a throphy.
Our chickens roast
Wid butthered toast,
I'm sure would timpt St. Pether.
Now you'll declare
Our bill of fare
It couldn't be complether.

CHORUS:
For we're the boys . . .

V.

Now silence all,
While I recall
A memory sweet and tender;
The maids and wives
That light our lives
With deep, enduring splendor—
We'll give no cheer
For those so dear,
But in our hearts we'll bless them,
And pray tonight,
That angels bright
May watch them and caress them.

CHORUS:
For we're the boys
That hearts desthroys,
Wid making love and fighting;
We take a fort,
The girls we court,
But most the last delight in.*

THE MIDNIGHT MARCH

ALL along the weary miles,
Down through the dark defiles,
Through the woods of pine and larch,
Under midnight's solemn arch,
Came the heavy, sounding march
Of the Seventh!

Scouts out on either flank,
Searching close through dyke and bank,
Sweeping with their restless eyes
Every hollow, cut, and rise,
Guarding from the foe's surprise.
All the Seventh!

Every pine-tree's jagged limb
In the black night looked grim;
And each dense thicket's shade
Seemed to hold an ambuscade;
Yet no soldier was afraid
In the Seventh!

Plod! plod! plod! plod!
Over gravel, over sod,
Over up-torn railroad tracks,
With their bending, belted backs,

* Frank Moore, "Poetry and Incidents," *The Rebellion Record* (New York, 1867), vol. I, p. 17.

Waiting—hoping vain attacks,
               Marched the Seventh!

"Halt! Rest!" along the line;
Down every man supine
In the wet gravel lay
Hugging with delight the clay,
Longing for the light of day
               On the Seventh!

Though the dark night was serene,
Never foeman's form was seen;
Though like flies they buzzed around,
Haunting every shady ground,
Fleeing at the slightest sound
               From the Seventh!

So we marched till night was gone
And the heavens were blessed with dawn;
But History, with immortal hand,
Must yet record how firm and grand
Was that march through Maryland
               Of the Seventh! *

CAMP CAMERON, *May* 9, 1861.

WEARING OF THE GREY

Who once has stood in the line of grey
   And marched to the rattling drum,
And heard the ring of the rifle sling
   As the crackling orders come;
And seen the sun on the breastplates gleam
   And the wind with the guidon play;
He has given his soul to the age-old role,
   To the wearing of the grey.

* *Harper's Weekly*, June 1, 1861.

So drink to the blue of the days gone by
  To the glistening whites for dress,
To the khaki too that the greasers knew
  In the dusty border mess;
To the olive-drab that broke the line
  To these—"Long Life!" we say;
And loud our toast to our fathers' boast
  To the wearing of the grey.

From the jungle green of the South Sea Isles
  And from Iceland's frozen lands,
From Britain's mighty battlements
  And Tunisia's torrid sands.
From land and sea and from the air
  We seem to hear them say:
"Now drink this toast to our Fathers' boast
  TO THE WEARING OF THE GREY."

Appendix III

Biographical Notes

MARSHALL LEFFERTS was born in Brooklyn, New York, January 15, 1821. He was a direct descendant of Leffert Pieterson van Haughwort who founded the family in America in 1660. He was educated at the County School and, at the age of fifteen, became a clerk in a hardware store. He soon left this position to join the staff of the chief engineer of Brooklyn, where he began to study civil engineering. Although he soon became assistant engineer, Lefferts was ambitious and needed a wider scope for his obvious talents. Thus, after three years of engineering, he took a position as a clerk in the firm of Morewood & Co., Importers. Within three years he became partner and, until 1852, active manager of its affairs. In that year he resigned to form his own company and engaged in the manufacturing of iron and the perfecting of a new process for galvanizing iron. Some years before he had met Alexander Bain, the electrical inventor, and become fascinated with the chemical telegraph. Joining with several wealthy New York and Boston investors, he organized the New York and New England and New York State telegraph companies. As president of the company he supervised the construction of a line between New York and Boston, and later between New York and Buffalo.

When these lines were consolidated with the Morse lines in 1860, he resigned but returned to the same field as electrical engineer for the newly formed American Telegraph Co. He was highly successful in this job and made the company one of the most efficient and best organized telegraph systems in the world. In 1866 the company was consolidated with Western Union, and Lefferts was chosen engineer. He resigned shortly after to establish the Commercial News Department of the same company. In 1869 he became president of the Gold and Stock Telegraph Co., which, shortly after, purchased the Commercial News Department from Western Union.

Lefferts joined the Seventh Regiment as a private in 1851. A year later he was elected Lieutenant Colonel and in 1859 became Colonel. At the close of the war he resigned and, soon after, was chosen Commandant of the Veteran Corps of the Seventh. On July 3, 1876, he suffered a heart attack while the Corps was en route to Philadelphia, and died within a few minutes.

BENJAMIN F. BUTLER was born in Deerfield, New Hampshire, in 1818, but moved to Lowell, Massachusetts, in his early youth. After graduating from Waterville (now Colby) College in 1838, he studied law and was admitted to the bar in 1840. He was elected to the Massachusetts House of Representatives as a Democrat in 1853 and to the state senate in 1859. Shortly after the events of April, 1861, he was given command of the District of Annapolis, and later of Fortress Monroe. In June 1861 he was defeated by the Confederates at Big Bethel and relieved of his command. Within a short time, however, he was put in charge of an expedition which succeeded in capturing Forts Hatteras and Clark on the North Carolina coast, August 27 and 28, 1861. Butler then returned to Massachusetts to organize a brigade that was to act as an occupying force for Admiral Farragut's naval invasion of New Orleans. He occupied the city on May 1, 1862, and remained there until December 16, when he was removed because of the criticism his highhanded regime had aroused. Among the notorious incidents of this period were the hanging of William Mumford for pulling down the Union flag from the mint, his "Woman Order," which earned him the title, "Beast Butler," and his confiscation of $800,000 which he claimed had been entrusted by the Confederates to the Dutch consul, for the purpose of purchasing war supplies. He also earned the nickname, "Silverspoon," for allegedly stealing silverware from Southerners. As commander of the Army of the James he was defeated by Beauregard at Drewry's Bluff and was removed from command after his blunder in failing to capture Fort Fisher. From 1867 to 1875 Butler was in Congress, this time as a Radical Republican. After two unsuccessful attempts to win the governorship of Massachuetts as a Republican, he was elected Democratic governor in 1882. Butler died in Washington, D. C., January 11, 1893.

THEODORE WINTHROP, a direct descendant of the early governor of Massachusetts, John Winthrop, was born in New Haven, September 22, 1828. After graduating from Yale in 1848, he was awarded the Clark Scholarship and spent another year in New Haven studying mental and moral science, Greek, German and History. Winthrop traveled in Europe, Central America, and in the western United States, gathering notes for the books on which his reputation rests. Although he studied law and was admitted to the bar, his first love was writing and he turned out a considerable number of novels and sketches, most of which were published after his death. He marched with the Seventh Regiment in April 1861, having agreed to furnish an account of the march to James Russell Lowell, who was then editor of the *Atlantic Monthly*. At Washington, he left the Regiment to join Benjamin Butler and was killed at Big Bethel, June 10, 1861.

FITZ-JAMES O'BRIEN was born in Limerick, Ireland, in 1828. During his years at the University of Dublin he began to display considerable literary talent. Upon leaving college he went to London, where in two years he dissipated his entire inheritance of eight thousand pounds. In 1852 he migrated to New York and soon became a general favorite. His most important literary contributions were for *Harper's Weekly* and *Putnam's Magazine*. He also wrote extensively for the stage. When war broke out he joined the Seventh Regiment but later resigned to seek active service with General Frederick Lander. He was killed in action at Cumberland, Virginia, in April 1862.

MATHEW B. BRADY AND THE SEVENTH. One member of the Seventh who was held in high esteem and affection by the Regiment during his entire life was Mathew B. Brady, the pioneer photographer of the Civil War. The exact dates of his membership have not been discovered, but he is listed as a member of the Veterans Corps in 1866. During May, 1861, he made a number of photographs of men of the Seventh and of scenes at Camp Cameron. The list of these is available at the National Archives. During his later years Brady was in desperate financial straits and his fellow-members of the Regiment came to his financial assistance.

Appendix IV

Tributes to the Seventh Regiment

FROM PRESIDENT JOHN F. KENNEDY

Lt. Gen. Edward J. O'Neill, Commanding General, First U.S. Army, delivered President John F. Kennedy's congratulatory message to members of the Seventh Regiment New York National Guard at the 643 Park Ave. Armory, Wednesday, April 19, 1961.

General O'Neill conveyed the following message during the regiment's Military Ball which was one of a series of events commemorating the departure of the Seventh to defend Washington, D.C., April 19, 1861:

"Your historic heritage as part of the defense of our Nation could give me many occasions upon which to congratulate you.

"I believe the one you are honoring on April 19th, the departure of your famous Regiment of the New York State Militia to the 'Defense of Washington'—is an appropriate centennial for us all to be reminded of the importance of the citizen-soldier to the security of the Nation.

"It is not insignificant that, according to your history, the famous regiment was quartered in the House of Representatives. As a former congressman, I feel that responsibility for calling forth the militia to execute the laws of the

237

Union, suppress insurrections and repel invasions, was visited upon the members of the House more dramatically at that moment than at any time before or since.

"You have my best wishes for a successful anniversary of your famous march to Washington. I know that now——as then—the members of the 'Militia' will stand to preserve the Union and the Nation whenever called upon."

P R O C L A M A T I O N

State of New York

Executive Chamber

In this year during which we begin to celebrate the 100th Anniversary of the Civil War, it is fitting that we commemorate a famous militia unit of the Empire State whose contribution to the winning of that war is unforgettable.

On April 15, 1861, President Lincoln issued a call for 75,000 soldiers to "cause the laws to be duly executed." On April 16, 1861 Major General Charles W. Sandford, Commanding Headquarters, First Division, New York State Militia, telegraphed Lieutenant General Winfield Scott in Washington, "The Seventh Regiment is ready and awaiting orders to proceed to Washington." On the following day the regiment received its order for embarkation.

On April 19, 1861 the Regiment, with baggage and artillery pulled out of Jersey City by railroad under the command of Colonel Marshall Lefferts, arriving at Philadelphia on the following day. Bridges and rails had been torn up between Baltimore and Washington. While the Seventh was enroute an enemy force from Baltimore had captured a train from Philadelphia and burned the bridges on the outskirts of Baltimore.

By means of a collection among officers and men, Colonel Lefferts chartered an old coastal steamer and sailed down the Delaware to Annapolis. Over the protests of the Mayor of Annapolis the Seventh Regiment landed at the Naval Academy grounds.

The Seventh Regiment arrived in Washington on April 25, 1861, thus effecting the relief of the Capital. This relief is one of the most remarkable and memorable events in United States history.

Thus the first militia regiment from New York State entered on its services. Of its members, 606 served later as officers in the Union Army.

In every subsequent war the Seventh Regiment has played a tremendous role. Its services to the cause of American liberty have been of abiding value.

NOW, THEREFORE, I, Nelson A. Rockefeller, Governor of the State of New York, do hereby proclaim April 19, 1961, as

SEVENTH REGIMENT DAY

in New York State.

G I V E N under my hand and the
Privy Seal of the State at
the Capitol in the City of
Albany this fourth day of
April in the year of our Lord
one thousand nine hundred and
sixty-one.

BY THE GOVERNOR

Secretary to the Governor

Bibliography

THE FOLLOWING materials were used in the preparation of this volume and constitute a reasonably complete collection of sources on the Seventh Regiment's participation in the 1861 campaign. The New-York Historical Society holds in its possession the military library of the Seventh Regiment, which contains a vast collection of manuscript material.

Butler, Benjamin Franklin, *The Autobiography and Personal Reminiscences of Major-General B. F. Butler: Butler's Book*. Boston, Thayer, 1892.

Clark, Emmons, *History of the Second Company of the Seventh Regiment (National Guard) New York State Militia, 1806-1863*. New York, Gregory, 1864.

Clark, Emmons, *History of the Seventh Regiment of New York, 1806-1889*. New York, The Regiment, 1890. 2 volumes.

Commager, Henry Steele, *The Blue and the Gray*. Indianapolis, Bobbs-Merrill, 1950.

Dalton, John Call, *John Call Dalton, M.D., U.S.V.* Cambridge, Riverside Press, 1892.

Higginson, Thomas Wentworth, *Massachusetts in the Army and Navy During the War of 1861-1865*. Boston, Wright and Potter, 1896. 2 volumes.

The Knapsack: a daily journal of the Seventh Regiment new armory fair, vol. 1, no. 1-18; Nov. 17–Dec. 6, 1879.

Leech, Margaret, *Reveille in Washington, 1860-1865*. New York, Harper, 1941.

Mearns, David Chamber, *The Lincoln Papers*. New York, Doubleday, 1948. 2 volumes.

Miers, Earl Schenck and Angle, Paul M., *Tragic Years*—1861-1865. New York, Simon and Schuster, 1960. 2 volumes.

Messages from the Governor of New York State. Charles Z. Lincoln, ed. Volume V.

Moore, Frank, ed., *The Rebellion Record; a Diary of American Events*. New York, Putnam, 1861-1863; Van Nostrand, 1864-1868. 11 volumes and supplement.

Morgan, Edwin Dennison, Governor. Papers on file in Documents Room of New York State Library, Albany, New York.

New York State. *Annual Report of the Adjutant General*. Albany, State Printers, 1894.

Nevins, Allan, *The War for the Union*, vol. 1, *The Improvised War*. New York, Scribner, 1959.

Nicolay, John G. and Hay, John, *Abraham Lincoln, a History*. New York, Century, 1890. 4 volumes.

Phisterer, Frederick, *New York in the War of the Rebellion*. Albany, Lyon, 1912. 3 volumes and index.

Scharf, J. Thomas and Westcott, Thompson, *History of Philadelphia, 1609-1884*. Philadelphia, Everts, 1884. 3 volumes.

Strong, George Templeton, *Diary*, Allan Nevins and Milton Halsey Thomas, eds. New York, Macmillan, 1952. 4 volumes.

Swinton, William, *History of the Seventh Regiment National Guard, State of New York, During the War of the Rebellion*. New York, Fields, Osgood, 1870.

United States War Department, *The War of the Rebellion: A Compilation of the Official Records of the Union and Confederate Armies*. Washington, Government Printing Office, 1880-1901. 70 volumes in 128 parts.

Winthrop, Theodore, "Our March to Washington." *Atlantic Monthly* (June, 1861), pp. 744-756.

Winthrop, Theodore, "Washington as a Camp." *Atlantic Monthly* (July, 1861), pp. 106-113.

Index

241

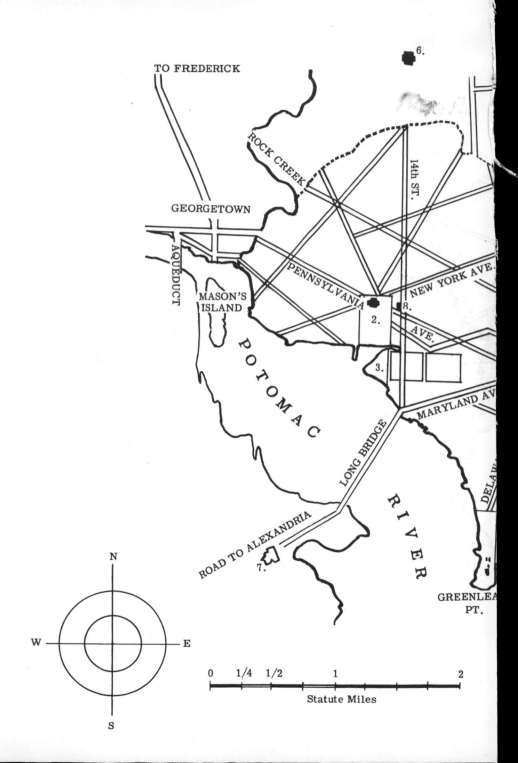

TO FREDERICK

ROCK CREEK

GEORGETOWN

14th ST.

6.

AQUEDUCT

MASON'S
ISLAND

PENNSYLVANIA

NEW YORK AVE.

2.

8.

P O T O M A C

3.

AVE.

MARYLAND AV

LONG BRIDGE

DELAW

R I V E R

ROAD TO ALEXANDRIA

7.

GREENLEA
PT.

N

W — E

S

0   1/4   1/2   1   2

Statute Miles